DUPL

D1293594

A CHRISTIAN PHILOSOPHY OF EXISTENCE

IGNACE LEPP

Foreword by
PATRICK MASTERSON

/ 00
LE

TEMPLEGATE   .   SPRINGFIELD, ILL.

First published in 1965

Translated by Lilian Soiron from
La Philosophie Chrétienne de l'Existence
published by Editions Montaigne, Paris

Nihil obstat: Eduardus Gallen,
            Censor. Theol. Deput.

Imprimi potest: + Joannes Carolus,
                Archiep. Dublinen.
                Hiberniæ Primas

Dublini die 28ª Junii, anno 1965.

Manufactured in the Republic of Ireland

CONTENTS

FOREWORD

The central theme of this book is to distinguish existential philosophy from existentialism and to vindicate its value for those who may be led to suppose that all existential philosophy inevitably involves atheism. The author shows that the exploration of the mystery of existence through an analysis of the various dimensions of human experience has been more effectively achieved within the tradition of Christian thought than by such acknowledged spokesmen of atheistic existentialism as Sartre and Merleau-Ponty. Thus the author confronts existentialism on its own ground and from its own perspective and seeks to show that even in this context there is a tradition of Christian thought which is more convincing than the existentialism which is indistinguishable from a thoroughgoing atheism. Indeed in his opening pages he provides a striking description of how contemporary atheistic existentialism, though motivated by a desire to transcend the false and dehumanizing absolutes of empiricism and idealism, has left in their place only absurdity and despair.

Dr Lepp devotes considerable attention to emphasizing that in contemporary existential philosophy the term ' existence ' signifies exclusively the reality proper to man. This explanation and the subsequent elucidation of the specialized usage of ' existence ' is of the utmost importance for a proper understanding of current existential thought. One may object to this novel use of terminology but one may not be indifferent to it. Unless the radical novelty of

existential terminology is appreciated, many who understand existence in a more traditional sense as the fundamental act of any being—the act which has its paradigm
expression in the divine perfection—will find themselves
arguing at cross purposes with existential philosophy.

Existence, as explained by the author, signifies the pro-
gressive self-realization by man of his human vocation. It
is the continuous and often anguished development of an
individual subject, worked out in a concrete situation
against a background of the past and a project for the
future. As such, existence is opposed to the closed and
strictly determined realm of material things or objects. It
manifests itself rather as dynamic subjectivity and situated
liberty. Authentic existential philosophy is never detached
and remote from existence itself. It is the intimate and
personal activity of an individual subject seeking a salvific
direction for his life through introspection and reflective
analysis of his own lived experiences. It is a quest for
meaning and value in the concrete exercise of his subjectivity. It is not a disinterested metaphysical system or a
Summa Philosophiae but rather a spiritual itinerary in the
tradition of St Augustine's *Confessions* or Pascal's *Pensées*.

In commending this intrinsically personal and authropo-
centric orientation of existential philosophy Dr Lepp
contrasts it with every other conception of philosophy,
describing them collectively, in a rather cavalier fashion,
as notionalism. It must be admitted that his sweeping
generalizations about the history of philosophy, though
sometimes suggestive, are often over-simplifications and
at times even tend to mislead. By notionalism he means any
philosophy which aims at an impartial, objective, and
universal comprehension of the order of being as it is in
itself. He implies a radical tension between philosophy

conceived as an objective and universal understanding of being elaborated through metaphysical concepts and principles, and philosophy conceived as an enthusiastic and personal programme for authentic existence mediated by the reflective analysis of a concrete and situated subjectivity. This implied opposition between traditional metaphysics and existential phenomenology introduces a certain ambiguity into his repeated insistence that existential thought attains to permanent, essential, and genuinely universal truth about reality, and that without this it would not be entitled to call itself philosophy. Perhaps his explicit assertions in the second half of the book that phenomenology must be completed by ontology should be understood as a genuine qualification of his earlier severe critique of traditional metaphysics.

His fundamental objection to atheistic existentialism is that it is not sufficiently existential. It confines the range of phenomenological description and analysis to the darker side of human reality, and arbitrarily dismisses as inauthentic all that is great, beautiful and generous in existence. Dr Lepp argues that authentic existential reflection must be open and attentive to every experience and dimension of human existence, including religious belief. We must consider seriously whether a comprehensive analysis of our human condition manifests the reality of a transcendent perfection as the fundamental theme and ultimate term of our aspirations. We may not dogmatically dismiss as bad faith or delusion the compelling testimony of remarkable men whose relentless analysis of their lived vicissitudes utterly convinced them that in God alone is to be found the ultimate meaning and purpose of human existence.

Dr Lepp indicates that in Christian thought there is a permanent and most convincing tradition of such existential testimony. He illustrates the existential viewpoint not merely of many contemporary Christian philosophers, but also of Pascal, St Bonaventure, St Augustine, and indeed the Gospels themselves. He underlines the recurring theme that the extraordinary syntheses in man of perfection and insufficiency, of transcendental aspirations and radical contingency, of concern and hope, impel us to decipher the sense and purpose of the human project as a vocation lovingly bestowed by a provident creator. The reality of God is affirmed, not so much as a theoretical necessity to resolve a metaphysical contradiction, but as a concrete exigency to render human existence meaningful or even bearable. The God affirmed by Christian existentialists is not simply the God of the philosophers, but truly the God of Abraham, Isaac, and Jacob, the God of Jesus Christ.

In the final chapters the author emphasizes that an authentic philosophy of existence is deeply concerned with the communal aspects of the human condition and is not, as many imagine, interested exclusively in the intimacy and subjectivity of the individual existent. The assertion that existence has meaning only in relation to Transcendence does not mean that religion is embraced as a comforting escape from the social problems and challenges encountered in concrete experience. On the contrary, because the affirmation of God is a radical vindication of the value of human existence and human aspirations the existential believer is constantly inspired and sustained in his endeavours to promote the fullest possible realization of genuine cultural values. Religion does not insulate the believer from the world, but gives him a true appreciation of his responsibility for it. Existential solitude and reflective self-awareness are not equivalent to distrustful isolationism, but rather a moment in a dialectic which culminates in authentic interpersonal relationships. If atheistic existentialism proclaims that solitude is the natural and most appropriate condition of man it is because existence for it is essentially egoism and not generosity. Such a contention cannot be supported by unbiased phenomenological analysis which reveals that human existence in its noblest manifestations is characterized by love, friendship, and communion.

The great merit of Ignace Lepp's study is that it shows how a Christian view of life corresponds more fully to the exigencies of concrete existence than the various versions of atheistic existentialism. In an altogether unique and transforming fashion the Christian message of divine salvation reveals a meaning and value in the hopes, aspirations and conflicts experienced in human existence; and of which atheistic existentialism fails to provide a satisfactory account.

One important implication of the author's account, which is not always evident, is that authentic existential phenomenology must transcend its inherently limited perspective and develop an appropriate ontology. The existentialism which seeks to confine the foundation and elucidation of existence exlcusively within the boundaries of human experience itself, is incompatible with the affirmation of God. The affirmation of a transcendent source of existence requires that we push beyond a phenomenological description of how the world and the self unfold in experience, to an account of how reality must be ordered in itself so that this lived experience should be possible. This metaphysical level of explanation is present in Dr Lepp's account but its distinctive character and significance is somewhat submerged. He is more concerned to emphasize the harmonious unity and compatibility of every feature of authentic human existence. The Christian existential philosophy which he describes is one in which the various aspects of existential experience, philosophical reflection, and Christian belief are indistinguishably fused in a comprehensive Christian conception of life.

Many, though favouring this ideal of a unified account of all levels of human existence, will nevertheless point out that the distinctive nature and role of the various elements involved must not be unduly suppressed. Lived experience is not identical with philosophical comprehension of this experience, and Christian revelation exceeds the scope of philosophical comprehension. The traditional questions and objectives of philosophy are not eliminated by adopting a more elastic and less critical conception of the nature of philosophy.

Thus, for many, the Christian vision of existence proposed by Ignace Lepp should not, strictly speaking, be called philosophy. It would be described as a coherent exposition in contemporary terms of a global outlook or way of life, which, though involving a definite philosophical intra-structure, is nevertheless specifically religious and theological. Undoubtedly many featues of this general world picture can be adopted as the pre-philosophical basis of a strictly metaphysical analysis. But this enquiry will be confined in its scope and its claims by the methods and evidence appropriate to such a specialized consideration. Its findings may be subsequently proposed as a real but inevitably limited confirmation of the believer's spontaneously accepted global viewpoint. Such a confirmation, considered as critical and metaphysical validation of the philosophical assumptions implicit in a Christian conception of reality, would, in the opinion of many, be a more precise account of the meaning of Christian philosophy.

At all events such strictly metaphysical reflection cannot be considered incidental to the development and verification of Dr Lepp's contention that Christianity is more authentically existential than the atheistic existentialism of Sartre or Merleau-Ponty. Albert Dondeyne, for example, has emphasized this point and illustrated the relevance of Thomistic metaphysics to the adequate elaboration of a critical philosophy of existence. Perhaps the most interesting feature of this book is that in freeing existential philosophy from the inadequacies of existential atheism, it provokes further reflection concerning the ultimate foundation and justification of an authentic and fully developed philosophy of existence.

PATRICK MASTERSON

University College
Dublin

Chapter 1

From Aristotle to Sartre

Western philosophic thought differs in its origin from Eastern, and particularly Hindu philosophy. I do not intend to enter into a consideration here as to whether the two main streams of thought were conditioned by the intrinsic structures of the one and the other ' world,' or whether these two worlds have become so different from one another because their respective philosophies diverged from their very beginnings. The fact remains that both Eastern and Western civilizations are shaped by their respective philosophies. This shows the error of a theory —more or less Marxist in conception—which was current in the early years of this century, and which considered philosophy as the futile verbiage of men divorced from all contact with reality, whereas the real basis of civilization rested on economic conditions.

The philosophy of the East, being based on asceticism and introspection, is clearly religious in its origin. Eastern thinkers concentrated on acquiring a knowledge of the self. They were concerned with the external world only in so far as it was an extension of this self. We in the West, conscious of our technical superiority, are easily tempted to describe Eastern philosophy as ineffectual. In fact, however, the effectiveness of this philosophy has been on a different plane. It is thanks to it that the East has acquired such a deep and extensive knowledge of psychology and of the human mind. Recent researches by Jean Herbert and his collaborators have given us a more accurate picture of Indian philosophical literature, and consequently of the accuracy of Indian psychological science. The functioning and motivation of the mind, which we are only beginning to glimpse with the aid of psycho-analysis and other branches of modern science, and which even the intuitive approach of our great mystics barely touched, have long been the subject of detailed study by the spiritual teachers of the East.

The earliest philosophers in the West were natural scientists. They and those who followed them aimed at understanding nature and the visible world which constituted man's environment. Each forward step in knowledge was consequently a progress in the science of nature. It was comparatively late before the Greek philosophers began to take an interest in man, and even then it was only from the point of view of defining his place in nature. Whereas the Hindu philosopher explores the relationship between the physical world and the soul, the tendency of Western philosophy is to reduce human quality to the level of the physical, and modern psycho-physicists still essentially follow the path first opened up by the Ionians. When Aristotle wished to describe ideas which could not be reduced to physical terms, he very logically invented the term ' metaphysics,' meaning that which comes after the science of matter. God himself is the ' first cause ' on the analogy of physical causation. Starting from these premises, Western philosophy has made enormous strides in the knowledge and consequent exploitation of the physical world; but where the mind and matters of the spirit in general are concerned, we must confess to a poverty of achievement whose seriousness, thanks to Hindu philosophers, we are now beginning to realize. The non-humanistic and materialist character of Western civilization is the logical and historical consequence of the materialist slant of our philosophy. In *The Sources of Morality and Religion* Bergson speculates as to the course our civilization would have taken if it had been based not on the study of matter but on the study of mind. We should perhaps have been saved from our soul-destroying obsession with progress as an end in itself, and it would instead have become a means to the attainment of man's true welfare.

In the evolution of philosophical thought Marxism first appears especially as a healthy and sane reaction against the meaningless abstractions of idealism. The direct consequence of the philosophy of idealism was intellectual anarchy, bringing in its wake a denial of all values, all beliefs, of eternity itself, as well as that withdrawal from reality which is equivalent to neurosis. Its object was to re-establish the real world and man's place in it. Marx hoped to substitute the concrete dialectic of historical evolution for the dialectic of the abstract idea taught by his master Hegel; but he was too much the product of his time to be able to achieve this aim. His faith in ' science ' —the science of the nineteenth century—was as absolute as that of the Greeks and mediaeval philosophers in the physics of Aristotle. Being an atheist, Marx took no account of man as a spirit, and saw him only as the plaything of economic forces. Far from marking a real advance in thought, Marx's philosophy was a return to the lowest materialism of Democritus, Epicurus, Lucretius, or some of the less intelligent scholastics of the Middle Ages. The dialectical—and necessarily idealistic—apparatus of his

2

theory, which he borrowed from Hegel, was intended to present Marxism as something new in the history of Western philosophy. The practical consequences of Marxism are at least as harmful to man as were those which derived from idealism. We may even say that Marxism, being an amalgam of the most abstract idealism and the lowest levels of ' scientism,' has built up a ' metaphysic ' which combines the errors of both.

It fell to a Danish contemporary of Karl Marx, Sören Kierkegaard, to achieve a genuine advance on the theories of scientism—whether physical, mathematical or sociological—and idealism in all its aspects. Kierkegaard, who died in 1855 at the age of 42, was almost unknown to the general public, and even to the intelligentsia, until after the First World War. Today he has become the acknowledged master of most of the Western philosophers. If the study of Hegel has had a revival, it is less thanks to Karl Marx than to Sören Kierkegaard. All the existentialists, no matter what their opinions and their internal controversies, derive directly or indirectly from Kierkegaard, who was the first deliberately to oppose existence to the abstractions of the logicians.

From childhood Sören Kierkegaard took a pessimistic view of man's condition and was a prey to remorse and anguish. Son of an elderly father who, though deeply religious, believed himself to be accursed of God, Kierkegaard continually meditated on Christ's humiliation and crucifixion. This was unusual in a strongly Protestant country, where the ' liberal Christian ' leaders of the Church valued the Gospel only for its moral teaching and the exemplary life of Jesus. Kierkegaard saw Christianity neither as a standard of ethics nor as a body of doctrine, but above all as a life with Christ. To be entitled to call

oneself a Christian it was therefore not enough to acknowledge the objective and theoretical truth of Christianity,
but to 'find a truth which for me is true,' that is to say,
a truth which becomes the very substance of one's being.
Kierkegaard's whole work amounts to a lengthy meditation
on the paradox of Christianity, for to him Christianity was
valid only because, and in so far as, it reverses all our
rational certainties and all our human conventions. While
the tendency of a liberal Protestantism is to eliminate from
the Gospel everything which apparently fails to satisfy
the criteria of reason, Kierkegaard insists on the inevitable
opposition between reason and Christianity. One of his
most important books, *Fear and Trembling*, praises Abraham's nobility and admirable faith in being prepared to
sacrifice his son Isaac, notwithstanding the obvious absurdity of such an act. And this not because Abraham was
convinced that it was God's will that he should sacrifice
his son. The whole glory of an act of faith evaporates if it
is to be based only on certainties. Man is never certain of
anything, not even of the faith which justifies and saves
him. All he knows is that he walks in the light of God, not
as a righteous man but as a sinner. Only when he recognizes himself as a sinner can he enter into communion
with God, the whole of Kierkegaard's dialectic being
founded on the acknowledgement of man's sinfulness.

The established State Church of Denmark was not, at
the beginning of the nineteenth century, inclined to accept
the tragic and tormented brand of Christianity held by
Kierkegaard. He consequently had to abandon his theological studies in preparation for the ministry, and even
to break with his Church. He might perhaps have been
happier in the Catholic fold, although at that date Catholicism was also more or less bedazzled by the famous 'light
of reason.'

Kierkegaard never intended to propound a new philosophic system. He waged war on all systems alike and particularly on that of Hegel, who stood highest in contemporary esteem. And as his contemporaries could not visualize a philosophy which was not systematized, Kierkegaard felt compelled to reject all philosophies in the name of existence. Every one of his books is the expression of his own personal torment, but it was no more than a personal reaction, and it would never have entered his thoughts that he should one day be considered as the founder of an important philosophical movement. The obsession of a divine malediction which oppressed his father, and the breaking off of his own engagement to Regine Oelsen, a rupture for no obvious reason and yet inevitable, were the two main factors in Sören Kierkegaard's life which had the greatest influence on his mind. While a certain joylessness, even melancholy, pervades his works, and his view of life is deeply pessimistic, this is not, as was later the case with some of his ' existentialist ' followers, because of any principles or preconceptions. His pessimism was derived from his inner life, and was naturally reflected in his writings. In such circumstances, we are tempted to wonder whether such a deep-rooted subjectivity can really be used as the basis of a formal philosophy; and indeed most of Kierkegaard's contemporaries would not have accorded him the rank of philosopher. Nevertheless, as I shall show later, the universal which is the concern of philosophy, is more truly present in the subjectivity of the extentialist than in logically impeccable abstract systems.

The nineteenth century and the beginning of the twentieth were hardly propitious to an understanding of Kierkegaard's existentialist revolt. Today we know that the apparent lack of concern for and the general want of interest in the problems of the inner life, which characterized most of the people of that time, were actually a form of collective neurosis. In the French Revolution of 1789 and the Industrial Revolution, men had been violently uprooted. Now they had nothing permanent to cling to, and professed to live by the light of reason alone. Religion and science were their only gods. Religion, in so far as it had survived the revolution, tended to be reduced to a simple practice of worship and to humanitarianism. The ecstasies of the mystics, the ' irrationalism ' of the saints, seemed to belong to another age, to the ' darkness of the Middle Ages,' which the ' modern ' believer unhesitatingly disclaimed. There were, of course, some noble spirits like Léon Bloy, Baudeliare, and other poets and artists, whose voices sounded a different note in the general chorus of a ' rational religion,' which incidentally owed more to Kant than to the Gospel. But how many heeded them?

It took two world wars, the proletarian revolutions of the twentieth century, the deadly class struggles, and the concentration camps, before modern man again began to query the foundations of the tranquil rationalism in which he had endeavoured to lead his life for more than a century and a half. Little by little he was forced to admit that science and material progress, far from creating happiness, only lead to suicide and a new barbarism. Psycho-analysis, for its part, revealed the hidden depths in man which were almost completely outside the domain of rationality. In this connection, it is particularly significant to note that Freud's original intention was to bring even the deepest recesses of the soul into the domain of reason, whereas the positive results of psycho-analytical research have been to emphasize the superficial character and the inadequacies of any purely rational science.

In Germany, the end of the First World War, and the fall of the mighty Prussian monarchy—that supreme incarnation, according to Hegel, of the historic spirit—inevitably led to the collapse of the over-elaborate edifice of superficial order and reason. The reaction against rationalism set in. Was not an occupied Germany, torn by revolution, a living demonstration of the bankruptcy of reason? The reign of the absurd and the irrational began to take shape. Martin Heidegger, a professor in Freiburg-im-Breisgau, was pre-eminently the mouthpiece of the defeat and despair of the German people. It was this very defeat and despair that the Nazi adventure claimed to end, but which in fact it succeeded only in intensifying.

Heidegger saw existence as a state of absolute dereliction. Man, not having chosen to exist, but still being obliged to continue existing, can have only a tragic destiny and awareness of misfortune. His realization of his existence coincides with another, and agonizing, realization: that he is cast into this precarious and inevitably doomed world to await the supreme and irremediable defeat of death. Man's existence is existing for death, and the only fitting act which he can perform during his lifetime is to acknowledge his nothingness and realize his existing for death in an original manner. The only real existence is that which knows itself to be absurd, fated to defeat in death, and yet has the courage to accept this. Those who do not dare to face the absolute emptiness of the human situation, who cravenly invent reasons for living, will only have an unreal existence. This is the lot of the great mass of humanity, who in order to go on living and working construct idols for themselves, whether they call them God, humanity, science or revolution. The illusion of a direction and purpose of existence is indispensable for the mass, but for the realist, the naked and cruel truth is sufficient.

We see that Heidegger, like Kierkegaard, denies the possibility of a rational optimism; he is haunted by the contradictions and miseries of the human condition, and for this reason his philosophy may rightly be called existentialism. Kierkegaard's faith, in spite of everything, cast a ray of hope through the darkness in which he struggled. But for Heidegger all was darkest night, for him there was neither God nor faith.

It is not difficult to recognize in Nietzsche, and also in Richard Wagner, the precursors of Heidegger's existentialism. The same torments, the same passionate negations, the same violent rejection of all clarity and reason, the same preference for night instead of day, are found in all three. Indeed Nietzsche had almost as much influence as Kierkegaard on the whole existentialist movement of the twentieth century.

Only one leading figure dared publicly to call in question the general optimism which prevailed in France during the period between the First and Second World Wars. This was Andre Malraux. Although he himself made no claim to be a philosopher, his novels and essays showed a better grasp of existentialism than that of most of the professional philosophers, including the ' existentialists ' themselves. He himself said, ' I am a writer. What other subject can fill my mind except man? ' It was, indeed, in order to describe man's existence in all its depths and miseries that Malraux traversed Europe and Asia, throwing himself actively into history wherever it was being made. Malraux could not see man as an abstraction, or an eternal essence, since his being is involved and only exists in the framework of a given civilization. Man's authenticity is measured by the degree of his participation in the realities of his times. Consequently he cannot pass through the world as a mere spectator, but must play his part in the great human drama, a spectacle whose varying but related acts present themselves in space and time.

Like all the existentialists Malraux sees human existence as an immense tragedy. The world that he loves is moulded in universal anguish and despair. In the long run all, whether revolutionaries, intellectuals, artists or adventurers, end by perceiving the absurdity of the universe, and realizing the abjectness of their own destiny. The most terrible reflection of all, for Malraux, is the thought that no matter what man does, he will never free himself from the exasperated feeling that this absurd, agonized and agonizing life is the only one, that never can he have a reasoned hope of another existence more consistent with the demands of his intelligence and the desires of his heart. This is because all existence must inevitably end in the terrifying reality of death, death which annihilates all that man could or would achieve. There are few writers and thinkers, not even Kierkegaard and Heidegger, who are so obsessed by the reality of death as Malraux. Indeed we can almost say that death is the protagonist in all his works. As soon as one of Malraux's heroes begins to reflect, he sees himself as doomed to die, and Malraux delights in defining man as ' the only animal who knows himself to be mortal.' Even the existence of a salvific God would not, to him, alleviate the horror of death, which relentlessly plunges us into the deepest realization of human powerlessness.

This is, of course, only one aspect of Malraux's fecund philosophy. The inter-war period in France was too unheeding, too foolishly optimistic, to pay any attention to the warnings of a novelist who visualized internecine conflict and suffering as the foundation of human existence. The horrors of war, concentration camps and prisons, which we have experienced since then should, however, have made Malraux the chief prophet of the tragic life of our times. But his refusal to make any concession to contemporary fashions, or to the ordinary and trivial, was the reason why the aimless youth of a troubled era did not take him as their prophet. Their spokesman was Jean-Paul Sartre.

I do not think it fair to make the author of *Being and Nothingness* responsible for the intellectual cult which the general public knows as ' existentialism.' With great dialectical power and by making a skilful use of the discoveries of psycho-analysis and the concepts of Heidegger, Sartre analysed in masterly fashion the phenomena of human behaviour, and the various data of consciousness. This has resulted, in spite of vehement protests from the philosopher himself, in the most despairing and the most pessimistic philosophic system known in the West today.

The most ordinary objects which surround Antoine Roquentin, the celebrated hero of Sartre's novel *La Nausee*, are incomprehensible to him, and fill him with disgust and nausea, because they have no purpose, no meaning. The trees in the public gardens do not desire to exist, have no reason for existing, but they cannot prevent themselves from existing. The same is exactly the case with man. In order to escape this nausea and the appalling conviction that he himself is superfluous in the world, Antoine Roquentin considers suicide. Even this, however, is no solution, for he would continue to exist in the minds of others, in the plants and vermin which would feed on his body. ' My death itself would be pointless, my corpse, my blood on these stones, among these plants . . . My decomposing flesh would be useless. I should for ever be in the way.' Existence is irremediably absurd. There is no way of escaping its absurdity.

Human reality, the ' for-itself,' with its radical freedom and its lucidity, offers no advance on the impenetrable opacity of the ' in-itself.' Man is condemned to freedom, exactly as the stone is condemned to be a stone. Our freedom is slavery, our conscience cannot be other than despairing, since there is no possible way out of its despair. Human consciousness, nothingness and facticity, knows that it is fated to abolition. The fundamental purpose of the ' for-itself' of human reality, is to become ' in-self,' that is to say solid and eternal, while still keeping the freedom and lucidity of the ' for-itself.' Such an ' in-itself,' ' for-itself' synthesis being impossible, man bestows an imaginary existence on it, projects it outside the empirical world and calls it God. One can thus say equally well that man is a ' project of self' or ' project of God,' as God is thus only the projection of man's unrealizable ambition. It should cause us no surprise, therefore, that man, the free and lucid ' for-itself,' should choose and adore a non-existent God. Choice and free-will being only one and the same reality (' Freewill is man's being,' writes Sartre in *Being and Nothingness*, ' that is to say, his non-being.'). It would be patently absurd, in these conditions, that this non-being should make any other choice than an absurd one.

It has been remarked that Sartre occasionally expresses the same ideas as some of the great mystics, who also considered man of himself to be nothingness. But, as Tauler has well said, he is ' nothingness capable of God.' awaiting God to fulfil him, while for Sartre man's nothingness is absolute. Sartre is in fact the first atheist philosopher of any importance in France who, far from exalting man, debases and 'annihilates' him. Was it not in order that 'man should be for man the supreme being' (Karl Marx), that the rationalists of the eighteenth and nineteenth centuries rejected God? The existentialist philosophy of Sartre shows that there is nothing noble in this man-without-God, and that he is only a wretched and unjustifiable absurdity.

Hence, according to Sartre, man must consequently realize his destiny apart from all absolute transcendence, all intrinsic or extrinsic significance of his existence. In *Les Mouches*, Orestes is the perfect incarnation of Sartre's ideal free man. He is 'free from all servitudes and all beliefs, without religion, without profession, free to commit himself to any thing and knowing that he must never be committed.' This freedom, however, which seems outwardly so complete, is not enough for Orestes, because to feel oneself free one must first be freed. Freed from what, since nothing binds him to anything? He dreams of a total commitment, so total that he can achieve the supreme detachment. In order to win this absolute freedom from morality, religion, country and his own feelings, he kills his mother, Clytemnestra, and her lover Aegisthus, and in so doing transcends anguish and remorse. ' When freedom has once illumined a man's soul,' Sarte makes Jupiter say as he watches Orestes, ' the gods can do nothing further against him.'

All the ' heroes ' of Sartre in *Les Chemins de la Liberté* are prisoners of their egoism, of their incapacity to put their freedom at the service of any worthwhile object. Mathieu affirms his freedom by basely refusing to marry his pregnant mistress; Ivitch, in order to feel free, denies herself to the man she loves and throws herself into the arms of the man she hates, while the homosexual Daniel marries Mathieu's mistress. Even Brunet, the fanatical militant communist, finally reaches the conviction that he too has made no valid use of his freedom, and that no cause is worth more than the worst betrayal.

The generality of men, too cowardly to live their ' freedom for nothing,' delude themselves with the illusion of doing something worthy with their lives, to give life a purpose and a meaning. One wants to become a great man, the second, a good man, and the third, a happy man. Now all these projects are only a camouflage of the absurd fundamental project of the ' for-itself ' which tries to become ' in-itself.' But just as man cannot become a god, so he cannot become a great or a happy man. The only ' fitting ' attitude with regard to existence consists in courageously accepting the radical divorce between man and the world, between what each of us expects from life and what life can give us. And this lucid view of existence requires the renunciation of any eternal ambition.

Sartre attributes the greater part of our deceptions to the ' illusion of seriousness,' and his chief grievance against Christianity is that it takes life seriously, that is to say as if life had a purpose and a meaning. Man being by his nature a nothingness, he can achieve nothing but nothingness, and all his efforts will result in nothingness. The abolition of this fatal ' illusion of seriousness ' is consequently one of the chief tasks of the existentialist doctrine of Sartre and his disciples. To scoff at all values, to respect nothing, whether love, religion, country or revolution—this is the mission of the true existentialist. Did not Sartre himself achieve the masterpiece of existentialism by writing several hundred pages to prove that the poet-thief-homosexual Jean Genêt was as much a saint as Saint John of the Cross? In *Being and Nothingness* he had already affirmed, ' There is no difference between the man who gets solitarily drunk and a leader of nations.' As man is ' for-itself,' that is conscience and freewill, the solitary drinker, drinking himself into a state of intoxication in complete freedom and total lucidity, is far more admirable in his drunken stupor than a chief of state in feverish activity, a prey to the deplorable ' illusion of seriousness ' which inspires him to believe that he is serving a ' great cause.' Only in so far as he shares in this ' illusion of seriousness ' does man condemn himself to despair.

In the chapters which follow, I shall evaluate the existentialist method of Sarte. The preceding pages will suffice to explain his extraordinary influence on a lost and unhappy generation. There is, however, no more dangerous error than to assume that existential philosophy is responsible for the aberrations of Sartre and those who are directly or indirectly his disciples, or to think that the reintegration of both mind and heart requires a return to an outworn rationalism whose excesses were in themselves the cause of the excesses of atheistic existentialism.

Chapter 2

Existence

The exponents of the absurd and of despair are far from being the only heirs to Sören Kierkegaard's existentialist philosophy, nor are they the most orthodox representatives of his ideas. Besides, Kierkegaard was influenced, knowingly or unknowingly, by a long tradition of Christian spiritual philosophy, a tradition unaffected by his death. However, before proceeding with our analysis of what has been described with more or less accuracy as ' Christian existentialism,' the reader is entitled to a definition of the terms ' existence ' and ' existentialism.'

The term ' existence,' as I understand it, does not at all mean the act exercised by any being because of its location in the time and space, which would be equivalent to recognizing equally the existence of a stone or a tree as that of man or of God. Heidegger calls this ' *Dasein*,' which may be translated as, ' being-in-the-world,' and he makes a basic opposition between it and existence. Man alone, of all the beings in our world, exists, and there cannot be any existence but his, since it is the distinctive characteristic of the human condition.

Existence is therefore radically different from the ' being-thing,' whether this is considered as material

' substance ' or as the ' being-in-itself ' of Sartre. It is also different from being as the spiritual ontology of Maurice Blondel understands it. Blondel, whose contribution to the renaissance of French philosophy is immeasurable, sees being as one, immutable, eternal; in other words, no reality in our universe is being except God alone. Being, however, is also action, and it is from this that the various and graded beings of the universe derive all their reality and their participation in being. Blondel's view of the being of man is not far removed from what we call existence.

Existence is not opaque and impenetrable matter which, as Sartre says, is crudely there—total, dense, massive, without any reason for existence, unrelated to any other being, superfluous for all eternity. And indeed it is true that, if Sartre's phenomenological description of the material being were not complemented by the spiritual ontology of Blondel, the universe would be absurd and without any reason for existing. It is only because ' matter is for life, life for the mind, and the mind for God,' that the lowest material being itself ceases to be opaque and impenetrable, and acquires its reason for existence and its significance. This does not make it in itself an existence, since existence, as we shall see, is essentially consciousness and freewill.

Since it is a characteristic of man, existence is neither eternal nor immutable. If pure being conforms to the principles of identity and of non-contradiction of traditional ontology, these are hardly ever applicable in the case of existence. As I have already written in *Authentic Existence*: ' Man is an astonishing mixture of time and eternity, of infinite and finite, of freewill and necessity, a mixture which is traditionally symbolized by the words " soul " and " body," or " spirit " and " flesh." Normally there is neither compromise nor harmony between these contra-

dictory elements which make up man, but a perpetual
struggle, in the course of which sometimes these and sometimes those gain the upper hand.' The phenomenological
method used by the existentialists teaches us that, for
existence, things are never quite what they seem. The
virgin is rarely completely virgin; the revolutionary almost
never completely revolutionary; and the conventional man
himself, too, is generally something more than a social
conformist. As Nicolas Berdyaev has said: ' Existence is
found in nostalgia, despair, excitement, non-fulfilment.'
But existence is also found in anxiety, overflowing joy,
enthusiasm, overwhelming passion, exalting hope. All this
is evidently neither the fact of absolute being nor of
matter. Existence is the being of man.

Some have attempted to identify existence with the
higher forms of life, life as understood, for example, by
Nietzsche or Bergson. These two philosophers did indeed
insist on the specific character of life, which the intellectual
climate of the nineteenth century tended to reduce to a
purely physical and chemical process. But while it is certain
that, by their courageous reaction against scientism and
rationalism, they contributed greatly to the climate which
fostered the flowering of modern existential philosophy,
neither Nietzsche nor Bergson were, properly speaking
existentialists, for the terms ' life ' and ' existence ' are
not, after all, synonymous. The intrinsic quality of life is
biological; its specific manifestations are social, whereas
existence begins beyond the biological and social, and
implies inwardness, intimacy and self-awareness.

According to Karl Jaspers, who has spent his life
reflecting on the problems of existence, what makes an
existence of man is not what he has in common with other
men, or even with other existences, but what is most

personal, most immediate and most intimate in him. As I myself am my subjectivity, I can consequently not have the same spectator attitude to it as I normally have to the objective world. The famous *cogito, ergo sum* of Descartes, the inference of the subject thinking of his existence, is a philosophical absurdity, since existence, being the material of the human being itself, cannot be rationally proved. Here scholastic philosophy confirms my thesis. It is agreed that first principles, that is to say, immediate truths, cannot be proved. The fact that many intelligent men at the beginning of this century could ask themselves, like Hamlet, whether or not they existed, proved how dangerously the philosophers had departed from the concrete and existential. It is true that to have immediate evidence of one's own existence, and consequently of the existence of others, one must transcend the banality of everyday and accede to authentic existence, and to succeed in this it is not enough to be a ' human reality.'

There is nothing more arbitrary, and nothing which more betrays a total ignorance of the subject, than the alleged opposition between existence and being. It is true that in contemporary terminology existence is not being, no more than it is matter. But neither is it, as Sartre holds, a negation of being. Unlike the absolute being and the empirical being (the *Dasein* of Heidegger), who are what they are and are susceptible of definition, the being of existence is never entirely given, complete; it is never being totally existing. Kierkegaard correctly understood the specific character of this being, so different from all other beings, when he described existence as ' tension.'

Existence is not, any more than being, opposed to essence. If it is true that existence is tension, excitement, nostalgia, despair, hope, suffering, joy and so on, it is not these things in a chaotic manner. There is a permanent core which causes all these phenomena, in spite of their multiplicity, to tend towards unity. It is significant that two existentialist writers, who were not at all influenced by Christian metaphysics, Andre Malraux and Albert Camus, affirm the reality of a human essence. Malraux sees the permanence, the continuity and the unity of man in the ' fundamental.' Alike in resignation as in revolt, in overflowing joy as in sharpest anguish, twentieth-century man, the soldier of 1914, the prisoner of 1940, the resistance worker of 1944, the Chinese coolie, the Spanish hidalgo, the convinced Christian and the anarchist, are linked, across the Middle Ages, with the first cave man. As for Camus, he attacks, in *The Rebel*, those who, in the name of historic opportunism, think they can ignore eternal man. The mistake of a certain theory of essentialism was to consider only the immutable aspect of reality and forget its dynamic character. Essences are not laid down in advance, but are realized in and by existence, without our having the right to speak of the superiority of one over the other. Creation is not a unique act which took place at the beginning of time, once and for all, and which time only makes real; it is continuous. At each instant, as Bergson so justly said, there is something previously unknown, something authentically new in the world. The Word which was in the beginning is not pure Idea, but pure Act. If, according to traditional Christian philosophy, essence and existence are only one in God, the essence of man becomes itself in existence. Should some existential philosophers seem to pass over this, it is because they have fallen into the error opposed to that of the essentialists, and do not see that, at the heart of existence, there is the existent.

Eternity is the duration of being, of God. Existence itself is temporal. Time for it is not an external objective means, but the very tissue of its interior self. The work of a philosopher like Bergson, emphasizing inner duration, enables us to understand what would probably have been somewhat difficult for our predecessors, if by chance they had asked themselves the same questions as we do. Jean Guitton, for his part, devoted the main share of his philosophic reflections to these problems of duration, and made an important contribution to the working out of a new existential ontology. If the philosophers of former times can be excused for having conceived evolution, even for man, as an imperfection, and having placed more stress on the static than on movement, it is because the knowledge which they possessed, did not allow them to understand time otherwise than as a sort of debasement of eternity, just as existence itself could only seem to them a debasement of being. Thanks to Bergson and to Guitton, we now know that time and eternity are two durations of different kinds, and the perspectives of the one are not necessarily the perspectives of the other. Existence does not tend to rest, to death, but to a higher existence. Consequently it is in time that man must accomplish the innumerable decisions which enable him to exist.

Existence not being one and harmonious, but multiple and divergent, cannot be the object of a definition, any more than it can be an object of science. Traditional philosophy, ambitious to resemble a science, did not always attain existential reality. In order to succeed, we must abandon deductive methods, and choose a new method, that of phenomenological analysis. Introspection is the first step in this method; and it is self-evident that for this we must use all the means that modern psychological science, including psycho-analysis and mystical experience, puts at our disposal. Next we must reflect on the various situations experienced, in order to deduce the general laws governing human behaviour. So that these laws may have the minimum amount of universal application which is necessary before we are entitled to speak of philosophy, it is obviously important not to restrict one's existential experience to situations that are either too few or too much alike. The most valid criticisms of Sartre's existentialism are precisely that he insists on limiting existential reflection to the darker side of human reality, and, without sufficiently considering the matter, refuses as inauthentic all that is great, beautiful and generous in existence. In these conditions it is inevitable that faith appears to these philosophers only as a variant of bad faith, and love simply as a disguise of hate. In reality the laws which derive from Sartre's phenomenological analysis have no existential value, since they do not obey the fundamental rules of the method.

The first truth which the philosopher discovers by existential analysis is that existential being *is not*, but rather *is-to-be*. It follows that if the perfection of being is found in its permanence and immutability, that of existence consists in the intensity of its becoming. Evolution is so essential to the human condition that death itself will not put an end to it; and even life after death will be a magnificent and continual advance.

Existential evolution should not, however, be compared to physical, biological or even psychological and historical evolution. Nineteenth-century evolutionism, giving credence to this confusion, could only result in the reduction of human reality to a fraction of the empirical world. Those who took the view that philosophy was out of date and useless, and who considered man as much an object of science as anything else, were, in these circumstances, arguing quite logically from their premises.

The evolution of nature proceeds automatically, according to the inherent laws of each being or group of empirical beings, or again under the impulse of extrinsic causes. Man, as an empirical being, akin to all the other beings in the universe, also obeys the laws of evolution. His bodily and spiritual growth, certain transformations which he makes in the circumstances of his life or in the society of which he is a member, belong to the same order as the evolution which has been observed in the animal or even in the vegetable and mineral kingdoms. But it is quite different for him considered as an existent, that is to say as a specifically human reality. Existential evolution as such is the work of man himself. It is impelled by and directed by what we call the ' existential project.' Existence does not accept itself as it is, but neither is it a blind force which controls that ' tension ' considered by Kierkegaard as one of the essential properties of existence. As soon as man sees himself as existent, he formulates his fundamental project to direct his aspirations and his future. As well as the fundamental project, each existent sets himself particular projects which are the more or less direct means of the realization of the fundamental project. According to Sartre, the fundamental project of the existent is to become a god, and since man can never become God, his existence can only end in final failure. His particular projects—to do something noble with his life, to love and marry, choose such and such a profession and so on—being based on the impossible and absurd fundamental project, can only end in similar failure. Here again we see, in spite of Sartre's vehement protests, how pessimistic and ' absurd ' is his existentialism, and this is due to the atheism of his postulates, which are completely unphilosophic.

A stricter phenomenological analysis teaches us that the fundamental project of man is the realization of his destiny. This, for me, and probably for the immense majority of religiously-minded people, consists not so much in becoming God, but in resembling God. Is this project incapable of realization, inevitably condemned to failure? That is the whole question. From the point of view of strictly natural existential experience, it does not seem possible to form any valid judgment in this domain. Whatever, indeed, the objective value of rational proofs for the existence of God, on the existential level they throw no light; and even supposing the existence of God to be proved, the problem before us remains the same. The question is whether or not man can find in God the full realization of himself. To answer this, we must take into account in our phenomenological analysis the religious experience of man, which none of the principles generally accepted by existential philosophers permit us to reject *a priori*, as Sartre and his disciples do. Now, this religious experience teaches us that man can effectively become more and more like God and, consequently, his fundamental project is not hopeless. This being so, other existential projects which inspire our ambitions are not doomed to failure either. It is true that they are not always ' good,' and we shall not realize them all but, in order that our existence should have a meaning, that it should be inspired by hope, it is enough that we should have the *possibility* of making it into something. On this point everyone is in agreement.

Existence, says Kierkegaard, is not a thing, but a task. It must invent itself every moment of its duration. If we do not take this task seriously, if we do not direct our ambitions, we shall become passively subject to the biological psychological, moral and sociological laws instead of using them towards our existential project. Instead of being masters, we shall become slaves.

Existential development is a perpetual conquest of matter by mind, since its effort moves towards a deeper and deeper spiritualization. It may be that, objectively speaking, contemporary man is not morally superior to his ancestor of ten thousand years ago. It seems certain, however, that for better or worse he is less guided by his primitive instincts, acts more with a view to his project; and this, in spite of everything, represents a specifically human progress. The state of innocence, if we understand it as Berdyaev does, as a state antecedent to the choice between good and evil, is pre-existential, and I find it difficult to give it any existential value.

In this perpetual becoming which is existence, there is no present which could constitute a stopping-point, just as there is no past which can be considered as something done with and classifiable. Our present is our constant effort towards the future; it is laden with the past, and transforms it tirelessly. Our changing the existential project is sufficient to cause the past also to change its purpose and meaning. Heraclitus was so impressed by the incessant evolution of all things, that he concluded that one never bathed twice in the same river. In the light of our analysis of existential becoming, we can complete this by saying that it is never the same man who bathes twice. And yet there is no break of continuity between the bather of yesterday and the bather of today, for man is his successive situations. As mind, he preserves the identity of his ego, not as an object, but as a subject of perpetual becoming. To understand how human reality can really evolve without ceasing to be itself, we must again turn to one of Bergson's concepts, that of creative duration.

Far from constituting the weakness and the wretchedness of the human condition, there is a true and authentic greatness in our state of incessant development. The Creator deserves no blame for not having completed us at the moment of our creation. Kierkegaard likes to quote Lessing's paradox: that if God held in his right hand beautiful and readymade truth and in his left, the painful and difficult search for truth, it is his left hand which he would open to those whom he loved. What is true of the search for truth, is also true of moral, intellectual and spiritual becoming. Refusal to acknowledge the laws of time, duration of existence, does not lead to eternity, but to death. There is nothing more foreign to existential views than ' opportunism,' whether it is intellectual, moral, spiritual or material. Beneath the appearance of plenitude, there is generally found only the suicide of existence. St Paul himself besought the Corinthians not to consider him as having reached the goal of Christian perfection, but simply as one who was still hastening towards it. Kierkegaard, who had such a strong appreciation of man's spiritual becoming, denied the right of anyone to call himself Christian. Christ alone is Christian, whereas the rest of us, on the most favourable view, are aspiring to become Christians.

It would be a great mistake to present existential becoming as being accomplished without effort and suffering, like the harmonious development of a beautiful flower. Have we not stated above that human reality is ambiguous, made up of contradictions and internal strife? It can consequently evolve only *dialectically*, through struggle and anguish. Each new situation, the birth of each new value, always implies the renunciation and death of what we were or had previously. André Gide's ambition

to possess all and to be all at the same time, is incapable
of realization on the existential plane, leading existence not
towards unity, but to dispersion and dissolution. In the
case of spiritual becoming, which is called conversion, the
' old Adam ' must die. We know from the *Confessions* of
St Augustine, and from the accounts of innumerable other
conversions, that this death does not take place without
pain. It is for this that so many men who admire the beau-
ties of the Christian faith, draw back before the decisive
step. Intellectual becoming demands, too, a laborious
discipline, which consists in casting aside all prejudice,
all ready-made opinions, all intellectual pride.

There is, however, no existence without becoming, and
it is useless to wish for its abolition. There are too many
examples of individuals and peoples who, through fear of
life, deliberately put an end to their becoming, for us still
to have any illusions about their fate. They are condemned
to atrophy, to death. They no longer create anything. On
the other hand, it would also be wrong to insist too
exclusively on the sorrows attendant on existential becoming, since the joys which it procures for those who live
intensely, compensate abundantly for the toil and suffering.

To use a term of Sartre's which has now entered into
twentieth-century terminology, but which is not always
understood in the same sense, existence is distinguished
from the empirical world by its quality of ' for-itself.'
This means that not only does it live, act, love, think, but
that it knows that it lives, acts, loves and thinks. We can
understand, consequently, that some philosophers have
made consciousness into the reality of existence itself. In
any case, even if it is certainly extreme to make the degree of
consciousness which we put into our actions the unique
criterion of existential value, there is still the fact that

only that which is conscious can have existential value. In my opinion, to speak as some psycho-analysts do of ' unconscious guilt,' is pure nonsense. One can no more speak of a fault or guilt which is unconscious than one can have an unconscious virtue. On the other hand, psycho-analysis can be a useful existential discipline, a means of enlarging the field of consciousness.

Existence, since the time of Kierkegaard—and, as we shall see, even before him—has always been considered as liberty. It was actually against the determinist prejudices of his time that Kierkegaard so vehemently affirmed the prerogatives of existence. It is incontestable that the determinist conception of human reality held during recent centuries, bears a heavy responsibility for the decadence of the West, and the state of discouragement and despair from which a large part of the younger generation is suffering today. As for the East, it is because its philosophy is determinist that they have never begun to make progress, and have lived for thousands of years in stagnation. The greatest harm done by pseudo-mystical determinism is found, however, in certain Christian milieux, where it has given birth to a false conception of divine Providence. Existence, as I have described it in this chapter and as all existential philosophers, ancient and modern, conceive it, can have no reality unless it is free.

Liberty confers on man the creative power which allows him to escape the mechanical laws of cosmic evolution, and to take in hand his own existential becoming. Every act of creation gives us the proof of our own liberty and of that of our fellows. The Byzantine controversies between the traditional advocates and opponents of human liberty can only seem to us like logistic gymnastics, without the least existential bearing. As I am certain of my existence, so I know I am free, since my conviction itself is an act of my liberty.

Man's liberty is not, any more than existence, a datum, an objective thing, something definitely acquired once and for all. It is because the traditional protagonists and opponents of liberty argued in the abstract and the absolute, that they could never agree, each remaining hopelessly enclosed in his own system, and it is for this reason that their arguments, on either side, seem to us so unconvincing. Just as existence must win over the objective world, so liberty will be a perpetual conquest of universal determinism. The one and the other, however, already exist, in embryo, in every being who comes into this world. The more we become human beings by transcending nature, the more we become free, without human liberty, however, ever being able to become absolute. Liberty will always be relative, relative to the entire cosmos, as to human society. Nature resists domination by man, other people appear primarily as an obstacle to the exercise of our liberty. It is, however, precisely because he meets resistance and obstacles that man realizes his liberty, and it is by struggling against them that he continually raises it to a higher level. Existentially, in fact, man is always free relatively to something or someone.

Existential freedom must not be confused either with the freewill of traditional philosophy or with arbitrary act, as some writers who were more or less influenced by Gide tend to do. Visualized as a power of choice between two acts or two things which are equally possible and attractive, freewill, in the strict sense of the term, does not exist anywhere. Man always has reasons or motives which guide his choice in one direction rather than in another. Thus when Christ was faced by temptation in the desert, there was no question of a freewill choice between the tempter and obedience to his Father. Yet who can deny the complete freedom of his loving submission to his Father's will? The same is true of the fiat of the Virgin, who was preserved by the virtue of the Immaculate Conception from all desire for evil, and the same will also be true for man entering, after his death, into the presence of God. His freewill cannot choose between God and a denial of God, and yet it is with sovereign existential liberty that he will love God through all eternity. As for the arbitrary act, it has nothing in common with liberty, since it is generally manifestly anti-existential and, in consequence, thus opposed to true liberty.

Liberty is such an essential human good that existence is not entitled to sacrifice it for anything in the world. It is true that abuses of liberty, on the individual as well as on the social level, are always possible. These abuses could engender anarchy and libertinism; but this is another problem, with which I shall deal later. For the moment the important thing is to understand that in sacrificing its liberty, existence does not protect itself from danger, but heads into the worst danger, that of its own destruction. The temptation which is so frequent with a great number of our contemporaries of putting the responsibility of their destiny in the hands of some tyrant or dictator borders on a neurosis, and is a sign of unforgivable cowardice. Order has no existential value unless it is the result of men's free consent. If, on the other hand, it is only obtained at the cost of sacrificing liberty, it represents the triumph of the forces of destruction, and it is the duty of any man worthy of the name to fight against it.

Since it is free, existence is not governed by so-called scientific laws. Even psychological laws, though more flexible than the laws of physics and mathematics, have only a relative bearing on it. Psycho-analysts and psychologists can certainly predict that a man with a given past and given temperament will generally, in certain circumstances, react in such a manner; but because of the creative power of liberty it will always be impossible to state exactly how this man will act or react. He can always, thanks to his liberty, take an original course which no science could foresee. Or if he did not have this capacity, it would prove that he was not a true existent, and that his liberty was still in bonds. Consequently, when I said above that existential reflection tries to discover the laws of human behaviour, I meant laws which are very different from scientific laws. Existential laws are not, as it were, a rigidly bounded canal, but the channel of a torrent; the water normally, it is true, keeps within its bounds, but, in time of flood, sweeps them away. Existential liberty, synonymous with power and the need of initiative and creation, cannot satisfy itself for any length of time within a rigid framework; sooner or later it will escape. Cowardly and timid people feel, more or less confusedly, that true liberty would prevent them from remaining static and mediocre, but would oblige them to a perpetual transcendence of self, exposing their life to risks. Consequently they are only too happy to barter it for any kind of slavery, to subject it to any kind of determinism. It is because psycho-analysts generally deal only with undeveloped, morbid people, that many have not yet understood the specific character of existential laws and speak of psychological determinism. A true man, on the contrary, develops in the midst of all the dangers and all the risks which the use of liberty entails.

Liberty and responsibility are two realities which are so firmly interwoven, that we are entitled to consider them as two aspects of one and the same existential reality. Besides, it is only because existence is responsible for itself and its commitments, that it esteems liberty so highly, and that it exists only in so far as it is freedom. But the idea of responsibility implies that of transcending, since a responsibility which is not a responsibility to someone superior to existence itself, is only an empty play on words. We can see this clearly in the case of someone like Sartre who, claiming to prove the absolute liberty and responsibility of man, ends in fact in the destruction of the one as well as the other. It is for this reason that the best existential philosophers attach so much importance to the analysis of belief or faith, which they rightly consider as a reality which is just as essential to existence as becoming and freewill. I shall, however, have occasion to deal with this at greater length when discussing the more specifically Christian problems of existential philosophy.

Chapter 3

From 'Notionalist' to Existentialist Philosophy

By traditional Western philosophy I understand here not a particular school or system, but a general tendency which originated with Aristotle and has dominated the teaching of philosophy for seven or eight centuries. Any other kind of thinking was considered as more or less unorthodox, or was even denied any title to be called a philosophy at all. This attitude still tends to prevail. In spite of the important differences which divide and alienate from one another the innumerable systems of what I shall call here notional or school philosophy, the name covers many of the mediaeval scholastics and their modern disciples: the nominalists, Descartes and the Cartesians, Hegel, Kant, Fichte, and all the nineteenth and twentieth-century idealists, the eighteenth-century materialists of the 'philosophy of enlightenment,' and the Marxist materialists, as well as the greater number of the philosophers of various minor schools who figure in the history of Western thought. A common characteristic of all these philosophers and schools is that they aim at objective, abstract knowledge. They observe existence more or less as the scientist does, that is to say, from the outside, endeavouring to put themselves as far as possible from it, for fear of endangering that impersonal serenity which seems to them an essential condition of all philosophic research.

The astonishing progress made first of all in the field of mathematics and then in that of natural science is due to this orientation of the leading Western philosophers. To it we owe the high degree of development attained by our material civilization, and a standard of living which is without precedent or equal in the civilizations inspired by other philosophies. But the concentration of Western thought on the objective and the rational has had other and less desirable consequences. It is also responsible for the West's current gross ignorance of and disdainful contempt for values and realities which are specifically spiritual and human. It is also largely to blame for the moral, intellectual and spiritual confusion so characteristic of our times. If we consider how well-informed most of us are about matter and energy, and compare this with the little we know about the mind and soul of man, we shall realize the terrible lack of balance in our ' humanism.'

It is not easy to find a common term to describe the schools of philosophy which we enumerated above. Since they all prefer the objective, the common and abstract to the subjective, the singular and the concrete, I use the word ' notionalism ' for this purpose. Although it is not completely satisfactory and only imperfectly conveys my meaning, I shall continue to use it here for want of a better term, it being understood that notionalists can be spiritualists or materialists, rationalists, idealists, empiricists and so on. They are only ' notionalists ' as such because of their common opposition to existential philosophy.

Nominalists like Occam, Hume and Berkeley, and idealists like Hegel, Kant, Fichte, Renouvier, Brunschvicg and others, are the two schools which have carried the abstract and objective tendencies of notionalism to the furthest lengths. But Descartes, whose ambition it was to remodel all branches of knowledge on mathematical methods, is practically in the same intellectual tradition. We may also include the materialism of Karl Marx and his disciples, since their ' man as an instrument of production ' is not concrete man, with awareness of self, but a simple abstraction, in the best traditions of the political economy of Ricardo and Adam Smith.

Notionalism, whatever its label and its particular aims, professes a real passion for abstract and objective knowledge. Its followers are generally most interested in the immutable universe of concepts and ideas, whereas the concrete world, which is a never-ending confrontation with self and in which nothing is ever perfect or adequately definable, seems scarcely worth their interest. It was always understood, and still is in the majority of text-books, that philosophic knowledge cannot apply to what is unique, singular and personal as such, that it can only deal with the universal and general. It is true that the majority of these philosophers do not dismiss sense-experience or empirical contact with tangible reality. But this experience and contact is, for them, a mere starting-point. Only when they enter the world of ideas, of ' being-in-itself,' do they feel really at home. To many of these philosophers, existence, taking place in time and space, partly subject to their laws, yet always individual and free, appears as something suspect, a more or less deplorable accident.

As I have already said, Marxism itself, in spite of appearances, and notwithstanding the vehement protests of its disciples, is an abstract notionalism. The revolutionary struggle is fought not for the welfare of actual and individual

4

man, but for the welfare of the proletariat. And for Karl Marx, faithful disciple of the idealist Hegel, the proletariat is an intellectual entity, having little in common with the proletarians of his acquaintance. Marx finds no difficulty, for example, in admitting that the workers of his time were, on the whole, dirty, lazy and unintellectual, whereas the sacred proletariat possesses every virtue, has no defects, and is entrusted with a grandiose historic mission. By following the same abstract dialectic today the Marxists think it quite normal and legitimate to sacrifice millions of real human beings for the abstract future welfare of abstract humanity. The dictatorship of the proletariat mercilessly destroys the proletarian.

Notional philosophers purposely ignore the real ' humanity ' of man, because they fear it, because this ' humanity ' is not susceptible to their methods of investigation and cannot be classified in their categories. León Brunschvicg specifically acknowledges this and counts it as one of the most praiseworthy features of his mathematical idealism. He reproaches Bergson and his disciples with being ' anthropocentric,' because they claim to establish a philosophy based on biological and psycho-physiological facts. It follows even more strongly that notionalists can feel only contempt, occasionally tempered with a little pity, for existential philosophy. As existence is freewill, it cannot indeed be defined in a ' clear idea.' It is outside the rules of formal logic and the laws of idealistic dialectic. According to all the evidence ' man-in-himself ' does not exist and man who does exist has no ' reality-in-himself.' Mathematical idealism being completely aloof, exempt from all contamination by man, appears to Brunschvicg to be the only philosophy worthy of the name.

The essence of man, as understood by notionalist

philosophy, is what is common to all men. Consequently, man as the subject of this philosophy, when defined by it as only a ' reasonable animal,' ' social animal,' ' producing animal ' etc., is an intellectual fiction, a simple concept, in which no one of us can recognize himself. As notionalist philosophy seeks theoretical knowledge, it must of necessity render objective everything it touches. But ' being,' made into an object for the purposes of study, is not existence, for existence must remain subjective, and cannot become an object without destroying itself.

Must we then conclude that notional philosophy is condemned and rejected without appeal? Some indeed take this view, and the younger generation, influenced by such criticisms as those I have just made, are quite ready to judge this philosophy as useless and even harmful. Such is not my opinion. I am convinced that notional philosophy has been and can be of great value for existence. It has fostered the creation of modern science and material progress, whose existential value should not be underestimated. It trains the reasoning power of the young by accustoming them to a certain rigour of thought which can never be considered as a bad thing and whose practical utility is incontestable. Formal logic and rational dialectic are themselves weapons which no educated man can neglect without serious loss.

I am consequently not opposing notionalist philosophy as such, but the use which has been made of it. It is particularly unfortunate that notionalist philosophers did not content themselves with theoretical knowledge alone, but attempted to apply to the realm of existence the principles which they discovered or elaborated, and to create a moral philosophy and a humanism. The arid morality of the nineteenth century, whose soporific influence is still felt nowadays in certain milieux, was very unjustly taken for Christian morality. It had its immediate origin in the pragmatic idealism of Emmanuel Kant, just as Hitler's concentration camps and the Bolshevist terrorism were perhaps excessive but logical applications of principles cherished by the rationalists of the last two centuries.

Notional philosophy analysed ideas, worked out definitions, drew up a logic and a dialectic; but it did not have the ability to understand the personal and concrete, liberty and life. As a result of its cult of the abstract, objective and general, Western humanity sacrificed the majority of the authentic existential values: love, faith, freedom, fidelity, flexibility, generosity, enthusiasm, passion, and so on. That a philosophy so destructive as the existentialism of Sartre could have so much influence on contemporary thought is not primarily the fault of Sartre himself, but of those who by their—conscious or unconscious—contempt for the realities of existence left a terrible void in the souls of men, to such an extent that the first who happened at the opportune moment to offer them food for the spirit, was acclaimed as a Messias, even though the food he offered them was contaminated.

The leading thinkers of the last centuries were unable to grasp existential realities. The greatest successes of notionalist philosophy were the amazing advances of science; but these undoubted achievements were unfortunately negatived, on the existential level, by the unleashing of blind forces. Just as objective knowledge was an end in itself for the philosophy which gave it birth, so progress became an idol for the whole of modern science. Instead of putting science at the service of existence, they allowed it to follow the laws of a mechanical evolution. Thus modern technology, making possible greater and speedier production, created a proletarian class; and the wonderful discoveries of hitherto unsuspected possibilities in cosmic energy were chiefly devoted to death and destruction.

The baneful effects of the semi-monopoly of notional philosophy on the minds of our immediate predecessors are seen at their worst in the world of religion. The great mediaeval scholastics took over the system of Aristotle as a weapon against the destructive rationalism of some Arabian and Christian philosophers such as Averroës, Avincenna, Abélard, Dun Scotus Erigena and others, whose influence on the universities seemed like becoming dangerous. The Church hesitated long before introducing rationalism into her apologetics, and only gradually recognized its usefulness. If things had stopped there all would have been well. Unfortunately, what was originally intended merely as a weapon for apologetics, tended to be set forth as an intrinsic doctrine of Christianity. The absurd discussions not only about the sex of the angels, but about the difference between grace which is efficient but not sufficient and grace which is sufficient but not efficient, and many other problems which had nothing to do with the Gospel of Christ, give a fairly exact idea of nineteenth-century theological text-books which reduced the Christian revelation to a series of logical demonstrations in which the Bible and the teaching of the Fathers of the Church figured much less than Aristotle, or even Descartes and Kant. I pass over those text-books of ' apologetics ' whose main effect is to repel any who take them up in the hope of finding the way to the living God.

As for the so-called Christian morality which was deduced from these abstract principles, and which had to suffice for generations of often heroic believers, it was seldom more than a system of natural ethics. As Holy Scripture was not much read in the nineteenth century, many sincere Christians would have been very surprised to learn that the morality which was preached in nearly all their pulpits, was inspired not by the Gospel of Jesus Christ, but by the *Critique of Pure Reason* of one Emmanuel Kant, the most abstract and least vital of all the philosophers. The fact is that for many years the main preoccupation of the majority of Christian moral teachers was to ' prove ' that the Christian revelation completely conformed to the famous ' natural laws ' so much in favour in the nineteenth and early twentieth centuries. In so doing, they believed themselves to be in complete conformity with ' Christian tradition,' not knowing, apparently, that if there is an exoteric Christian tradition, there is also an esoteric one for those who seek in Christianity something more than a conformity with natural laws or the rules of the schools of philosophy.

In these circumstances, it is not surprising that the Christian religion lost its unique and disconcerting character. Priests trained in these principles became respectable ecclesiastical civil servants; the Christian ideal sank to the level of the ' right-thinking man ' in perfect conformity with his social group, and in any case much closer to the teachings of the Stoics or of Kant than of those of the Gospel. Christianity thus ceased to be the leaven of the people. The force of inertia, resulting from original sin, debased it; and it became only a sort of social ethic, making use of promises of heaven and the threats of hell to preserve the established order, which in any case was not intrinsically Christian. The ' bourgeois,' that is to say the typical well-adapted citizen of the times, wanted religion for his wife and children so that they should be ' good,' religion for the masses to keep them quiet, while he himself put in an occasional appearance at Mass on Sundays to set a good example. To such a man the visions of the mystics, the altruism of the saints could only appear as irrationalities of another age, which had no place in ' enlightened Christianity,' the main concern of which was that there should be no visible difference between its followers and those who disowned Christ. Good manners demanded that the Christian should never give offence, that he should conform perfectly to the non-Christian world, and should overlook the beatitudes of the Sermon on the Mount, the summons to self-transcendence and to the greatness of the Apostles, the Fathers of the Church and the great mystical writers. It would be amusing, were it not so depressing, to quote at length from the majority of the ' commentaries ' on the Gospels, some of which date back less than thirty years, in which the commentator uses his best ingenuity to explain away the apparently scandalous words of Christ. Everything can and should be understood in a reasonable manner; the ' eye of the needle,' for instance, through which it is harder for a camel to pass than for a rich man to enter the Kingdom of Heaven, was not literally the eye of a needle but a gate in Jeruaslem, etc. etc. I know a convert to Christianity who, when he read one of these commentaries, no longer understood what the Gospel was about. If Jesus was indeed a respectable Jewish citizen like all his fellows, if there was nothing in his teaching to give offence to the Pharisees and hypocrites, to shake the slothful and the conformists, how was it that he was not received with open arms, but rather persecuted and crucified ?

It was logical and inevitable that the masses, who had nothing to hope from the established order so bitterly defended in the name of Christianity, should break away from it. Nor, considering the monstrous deformation of the Christian message, should we be surprised that a genius like Nietzsche believed that ' the death of God ' was a prerequisite of man emerging triumphantly from the appalling mediocrity into which he had been dragged by a so-called Christian, but in reality bourgeois and rationalist civilization. Were it not for the violent ' existentialist ' reaction of recent years, which had sporadic beginnings in the nineteenth century, the de-christianization of the West would probably be an accomplished fact today. In any case, not even the most subtle apologist can deny that in the hearts of the majority of our contemporaries in traditionally Christian countries, God is in fact dead and buried. Convinced rationalists like Renan and Taine, for example, who foretold the approaching end of Christianity, were incomparably more logical than the ' Christian ' theologians, moralists and apologists who ' proved ' the truth of Christianity and the excellence of Christian morality also by rational and scientific arguments.

Existential philosophy does not challenge the value of reason. It is not anti-intellectual, as has unfairly been alleged (perhaps because of the intemperate language of some of its less articulate disciples). True, as I have said in the previous chapter, the first and basic step of existential philosophy is not logical reasoning but direct contact, through introspection, with the actual situation. We do not, however, content ourselves with vague sensations and impressions. The second and equally necessary step in the phenomenological method used by existential philosophers is reflection on the situation which introspection has revealed. This reflection must use all the faculties, all the resources of the intelligence and even of dialectic reasoning to arrive at a philosophy. If sometimes we more or less distrust reason—and Kierkegaard, like Pascal before him, even openly denounced it—it is only because we are, consciously or unconsciously, reacting against the wrongful use of reason by notionalism. The existential thinker seeks reality with his whole self, and this self includes not only his reason, but his freedom, his ' heart,' his will, his senses, his instincts and, of course, his intelligence too. There should be no difference, where he is concerned, between philosophizing and existing; his philosophy is the fullest possible expression of his act of existing.

To grasp the extent of the gulf which divides an existential philosopher from a philosopher of pure concept and idea, we should not oppose a philosophy of ' sentiment ' or intuition to a philosophy of reason, but consider all that constitutes the difference between a man who lives in the real sense of the word and a professor who does nothing but lecture. The typical professor, the ' good professor ' so beloved of the lay universities, teaches everything which is in the programme, avoiding as far as possible any mention of his own convictions, preferences and involvements. His ideal is absolute objectivity, complete neutrality and identification with his text-book. The professor may of course have a sick wife or child at home, go to the mosque on Fridays or mass on Sundays, belong to a conservative, reformist or revolutionary political party, be a member of a literary or sports club. His pupils and readers need know nothing of all this in order to follow his teaching. Because for a long time the universities had only professors of philosophy like these, the man in the street visualizes a philosopher as a being who lives completely apart from time and space, understanding nothing of the happenings of daily life, taking no part in the sorrows, joys and struggles of ' ordinary ' humanity—a man who lives only in a universe of abstract ideas and problems unrelated to the concrete world. When Emmanuel Kant allowed himself to betray a momentary emotion on hearing the news of the French Revolution, it was an anomaly, one of these inexplicable ' errors ' which even the ' greatest ' men commit. The ' real philosopher ' was of course bound to be eccentric.

Unlike the professor, the existent, even if he too is a professor, can speak and write only at the prompting of his deepest self. Knowing himself to be charged with a message, he cannot keep silent. He may indeed be mistaken as to the objective value of his message, taking for absolute what is only relative; but is it not the essence of existence to be incomplete, subject to ' becoming ' as much on the plane of feelings as of intellect? Even if he is in error, what he writes or says has such an accent of sincerity and authenticity and such a power of persuasion, that his hearers or readers can never remain unmoved. Whereas to the notionalist thought alone counts, to the existent thought cannot be separated from existence itself. The books and speeches of existential philosophers are not about theories and laws of knowledge, structure of the soul or reason, the presence of which can be affirmed on grounds of logical deduction alone. They bring us face to face with men who live, fight, love and suffer.

As he is personally caught up in the drama of existence, the existential philosopher can obviously not look at it with the cold objectivity of a scientist or a theoretician. He will necessarily be subjective, passionate and partisan. And he will do this deliberately and knowingly, because his philosophy aims at being the transfiguration of reality and not a simple description. It is consequently not by pure chance that the leading existential thinkers, past and present, are found in the vanguard of the spiritual conflicts of their time. St Augustine was a great bishop and an unwearying fighter for the purity of his creed. Most of his books are polemics. Blaise Pascal was not only the author of the *Pensées*, but of that searing pamphlet known as *Les Provinciales*. I have already recounted the conflicts between Sören Kierkegaard and the established church of Denmark, corrupted by rationalist liberalism. As for our contemporaries, we know that neither Heidegger, Jaspers, Sartre, Merleau-Ponty, Camus, Malraux nor Gabriel Marcel held themselves aloof from our current struggles and anxieties. This obviously does not mean that they were all to be found in the same camp, since (contrary to the notion of Francis Jeanson, Sartre's young disciple) existential phenomenology does not in any way impose on its adherents the opinions of his master. The main characteristic of all existential philosophers, no matter what their other convictions or commitments, is that none of them considers the world as an object to be observed and studied from outside, but rather as something which conditions and consequently forms part of existence. They do not regard the world from an ivory tower, as scientists are bound to do, but they immerse themselves in its intimate rhythms. If we liken the behaviour of the notionalist philosopher to that of the scientist, we may say that the existential philosopher sees life in the same way as an artist does, and like him must in some way identify himself with nature.

Existential philosophy has no particular admiration for the famous ' clear thinking ' which has been considered, since the time of Descartes, Voltaire and Condillac, as the chief glory of French philosophy. If truth were known, these ideas are symptomatic of the serious disease which has afflicted French thought for more than three hundred years, and which has enclosed it in a strait-jacket of rationalism, depriving it of all capacity to understand deep human reality. Reality is neither clear nor simple, and we can only reduce it to clarity and simplicity by using the method of abstraction. By so doing we tend to overlook all that is individual, profound and mysterious in reality. To define man as a rational animal, for instance, certainly gives us a clear idea of him, though it is not as obvious as one might think, and in any case it teaches us little about Jones, Smith and Robinson.

We can consequently hardly blame existential philosophers for feeling a sort of instinctive repulsion when they are asked—as often happens—to define existential reality or existential philosophy. They should never be asked to say ' in a few words ' what they understand by existence. To define means taking the characteristics common to the kind or species, whereas existence, as we have seen, is neither a kind nor a species, and begins precisely where the common characteristics leave off. The phenomenological method which all existential thinkers use is not deductive, but analytical. It does not proceed by demonstrations and definitions, but aims at attaining reality as a whole by describing it. Bergson, who was more a philosopher of life and the vital force than of existence, was well aware of the superiority of the descriptive method, the only one capable of characterizing the individual and the concrete. Many existentialist philosophers like, occasionally at any rate, to use literary vehicles which are more flexible than the conventional philosophical treatise. They are novelists, playwrights, journalists, besides being philosophers. If Sartre had only written his monumental *Being and Nothingness* and his other strictly philosophical books, it is probable that he would never have become famous. It was *La Nausée*, *Huis-clos*, *Les Mouches* and *Les Chemins de la Liberté* which popularized the ' absurdity ' of existence, and *Being and Nothingness* should be considered as a sort of translation into so-called philosophical terminology of the existentialist situations described in his novels and plays. It is important to stress that this recourse to literature is not, from an existentialist point of view, a base or contemptible stratagem, for it is characteristic of existentialist philosophy not to limit itself to discussions between professional philosophers, but to be a call to conversion and to action. The most powerful existentialist atheistic thinker of our times, André Malraux, wrote practically nothing for a long time except novels. If the influence of Maurice Merleau-Ponty is very small beside that of his friend Sartre, although Ponty is incomparably his superior in intellect, it is because the former has not written any work of fiction. It is true, of course, that he took up journalism, which enabled him to be an existentialist philosopher, and not only a professor of existentialist philosophy.

We have already seen that the concept of man, as elaborated by the various schools of notionalist philosophy, is not the complete account of any one real man. I cannot fully recognize myself in any of the classic treatises on man, nor can I fully recognize the actual man who is my friend or in whom I am interested.

Let us take, on the other hand, two ' anthropological treatises,' less treatises than models for all existential philosophy: the *Confessions* of St Augustine and the *Pensées* of Blaise Pascal. The man whose spiritual adventures are described by these two great thinkers and writers is not a ' man-in-himself,' an objective and abstract man.

The man whose temptations and sins, whose search for truth and nobility, are avowed by Augustine is none other than Augustine himself, Augustine of Thagasta, later Bishop of Hippo. The man whose wretchedness and greatness is revealed by Pascal is a certain Blaise Pascal, a clearly-drawn personality, who cannot in any way be reduced to a so-called general definition of the average man. In the same way the almost pathological anguish which Sören Kierkegaard esteems one of the principal character-istics of existence is not a clinically observed, impersonal anguish; it is his own anguish, the anguish of a man who from his early youth was torn between the tragic and terribly harsh Christianity inherited from his father, and his strong desire for freedom. These three writers have this fundamental subjectivity which leads them basically to describe themselves alone, and gives to their work a vibrant emotional quality and a unique appeal. The human-ism of the notional philosophers who were wedded to objectivity—from Aristotle to Kant and Brunschvicg, via the mediaeval scholastics and the Cartesians—seems largely irrelevant to our modern world. Fifteen hundred years have passed since Augustine wrote his *Confessions*, and three hundred since Pascal confided his *Pensées* to paper, yet neither the one nor the other has faded. They are still read in every country, in every language, even by those who do not share the faith which inspired Augustine and Pascal. I myself have seen a young Chinese student, a Buddhist, reading St Augustine in his own tongue, and heard him speak enthusiastically of the acute analysis of the human soul by the great Christian doctor of Africa. The most significant fact is surely that the books of Augus-tine, Pascal and Kierkegaard are not read in the same way as the scholar studies documents whose only interest is historical or literary. They are seized on with passion, with partisanship, by the pilgrim searching for a lamp to light the road on which he travels.

This shows that each one of us feels a certain kinship with these extraordinary and extremely subjective beings such as Augustine, Pascal and Kierkegaard, rather than with learned and inevitably abstract and general definitions. Far removed as we may be from these exceptional men, all that is best in us makes their struggle ours; their ' confession ' of heights and depths, their hopes and despair make us more aware of our own situation in the world. A new concrete, existential ontology is in process of being created and, in my opinion, its philosophical value will be much superior to that of an ontology based on abstract and objective speculations.

It seems to me, then, proved that by interesting ourselves (in a more than purely rational way) in individual and concrete existence, in the 'being-in-situation,' that we have the best chance of finding the eternal and universal being, of becoming capable of communicating with the absolute Being. If I seek to know a being, I should not be asked to strip off all his individual characteristics by reducing him to a common denominator, a denominator which will necessarily be weak and void. On the contrary, I should treat him not as an object external and foreign to myself, but as a subject, an existent, with whom I shall try to realize an inter-subjective communion. By limiting our knowledge of our fellowman to what he may have in common with all men or with a given social group, we shall certainly know some things about him, for instance some qualities of his character or temperament, or again the colour of his skin or hair. But what do we know, for instance, about Richard Wright, who is probably the most brilliant of the younger generation of American novelists, by stating that he is a Negro from the Southern States, that he had an unhappy childhood and suffered through racial segregation? These statistical data are equally applicable to countless other American Negroes. It is only by taking Wright in himself, by entering into communication with his unique individuality, that we shall be able to know what he is, what constitutes the greatness and the weakness of his genius.

It is because the modern world, owing to centuries of rationalism, is objective in the extreme, that we have seen the birth of chauvinism, racialism, the fanatical class or caste spirit, so much opposed to the general characteristics of a civilization which has more and more taken on cosmic dimensions. Our French petit-bourgeois, for example, who thinks he has a complete explanation for the vast contemporary problem posed by the communist revolution when he says that it is a specially Slav problem (probably he knows nothing about the Slavs except a few clichés taken from obscure chauvinist journalists), and that it could not happen to ' people like us,' shows not only his crass ignorance, but also his fundamental inadaptation to the world in which we live. When the psycho-analysts take more interest in collective psychology, they will be able to write fascinating studies on the neuroses of this same petite-bourgeoisie, a class which history already seems to have passed by, but which still thinks itself guardian of the world conscience. There is nothing more repugnant to the existential viewpoint than police methods, unfortunately still in use in every-day life and in personal relationships, which tend to make out an anthropometric index card for every individual. As a matter of fact, as long as we only know what is objective and classifiable in a man, we shall not be far wrong in saying that we do not know him at all.

Nobody will deny that it is more difficult to elaborate a philosophy of existence, that is to say of inwardness and subjectivity, than the well-constructed systems of the notionalists of all schools. It is not easy always to keep one's mind young and flexible, to seek truth with passion even at an advanced age, to be ready ever to involve oneself afresh in the moving web of history. Our natural laziness tempts us to entrench ourselves in the repetition of theories which once upon a time we believed to have proved valid. Our ' disciples ' themselves—pupils and readers—demand that we should provide them with coherent systems, a ' summa ' giving a general view of all the problems that man's mind can possibly propound. In the Middle Ages, it is true, some great intellects were able, in good faith, to believe in the ' summae ' and ' specula ' which then abounded. Even Bossuet, in his day, could compose his discourse on ' universal history.' The present extent of man's knowledge, however, cannot legitimize such claims. Consequently philosophers who realize the transitory character of existence, and for whom all that is created must unceasingly be put in question, are even less entitled to make any such claim.

It is true that Heidegger, Jaspers and Gabriel Marcel thought they could elaborate existential *systems*, and it is very probable that these will be indispensable to existential philosophy in the creation of a new ontology. What is not permissible however is that some ' existentialists,' contrary to the fundamental postulates of the phenomenological method which is our standard, should claim to build their philosophy into a system. The day when Sartre and his partisans proclaimed that there could not be any ' existentialisms ' other than their own, they ceased to be philosophers of existence, and became as sectarian as those against whom Kierkegaard fought. We can consequently understand why real existential philosophers like Gabriel Marcel do not wish to be called ' existentialists,' since they have nothing in common with Sartre's dogmatism, and since the general public, knowing nothing about existence and what a philosophy of existence should be, takes Sartre's theories for the final form of existentialism, and concludes that any other existentialism must necessarily resemble it in some way. The Catholic Church itself, by warning Catholics in the encyclical *Humani Generis* against the spiritual and moral dangers of existentialism, is considering it as it is understood by the man in the street.

Since existential reality is perpetually, freely and ambiguously evolving, the philosophy which proposes to study it should not claim the pseudo-coherence of the notionalist philosophers. As I said earlier, existence and existential philosophy should not be separated, as object and subject are separated. If we were not slaves to certain habits of speech, we should never even add the suffix '-ism' to ' existence,' for as soon as we think of existential philosophy on the lines of idealism, materialism, etc., we are already taking leave of the true existential perspective. It is for this reason that I have preferred, in this essay, to speak of ' philosophy of existence ' rather than ' existentialism.' If I sometimes use the latter term, it is understood that it is always in an anti-systematic sense, without precise reference to any special ' existentialism.'

Another too common error about the philosophy of existence consists in considering it as fundamentally narcissist, based on the inner experience alone of an isolated subject, encased in solitude. When I wrote recently of the path which leads the being-in-situation, to the universal being, and quoted the example of the American Negro

writer Richard Wright, I may have risked giving some
readers the impression of advocating a farouche individualism, of recognizing only the individual man as an existential
reality. This is not so. Existence, at the same time and as
much as inwardness, is communion. My personal experience is only truly existential if it includes—always from
inside, by means of communion—the intimate experience
of other beings. Moreover, it is only thanks to others that
I am myself. The historical, geographical and sociological
circumstances of my birth and my life; the people I meet
daily, the prejudices, beliefs and the whole objective
ensemble that the Freudians call ' super ego ' are an integral
part of my existential situation. If it is true that we know
nothing about Richard Wright by reading his anthropometric statistics, it is also true that the circumstances of
being born in a Negro community in the Southern States,
of having known wretchedness and persecution, are indispensable factors of the direction taken by the very personal
genius of the writer.

   In order that ' existentialism ' should be entitled to call
itself a philosophy, it must transcend the individual
phenomenon to attain the permanent essence of the
spiritual being. Consequently, the ' existentialist ' is not
entitled unfairly to restrict the field of his experiences.
The existentialism of Sartre has given rise to a fundamentally pessimistic and ' absurd ' conception of human
reality because this philosopher, for reasons which his own
existential psycho-analysis reveals, wanted existential
communion only with sub-men, those whom he himself
calls ' depraved.' It is because he apparently did not want
to enter into communion with authentic existents that he
erroneously reduces authentic existence to inauthentic,
places bad faith above good, duplicity before sincerity,

hate before love. A correct phenomenological method demands that we should proceed as a scientist does. In order that the researcher may deduce scientific laws from his observations, he is bound to observe as many and varied facts as possible. We should do the same. Only a profoundly flexible thinker can become a philosopher of existence. He must give himself wholly to existence, free himself from all theoretical prejudices and all rational postulates. Consequently those existentialists who deny any existential authenticity to religious belief because of postulates cherished by atheist rationalism, are gravely disloyal to that phenomenological method to which they profess allegiance. Even if they had not been privileged to have a personal religious experience, nothing entitles them to reject *a priori* as invalid the testimony of many authentic existents who, according to all evidence, have known this experience.

I have written at length about the character of the perpetual becoming of existence. It follows that the philosophy of existence cannot take on itself to define or describe human reality statically. As it is a philosophy of human destiny, what is important to it is to discover the conditions which permit destiny to be realized, to attain to what we call authentic existence. To take a specially characteristic example, what interests us is not so much to know what Christianity is—although that also is important in our eyes—as to know how one can become Christian. To proclaim the supremacy of the salvation of man over the knowledge of things, however one understands the meaning of the term salvation, is the aim which all ' existentialists ' have given themselves. Even Heidegger and Sartre, though completely alienated from any spiritual concepts, are philosophers of salvation, and much more so than some very sincere believers whose philosophy is ' notionalist.' The important thing for the existentialist is to discover the meaning of existence, its origin, justification and purpose. We should not be surprised, accordingly, that for centuries it was Christian thinkers above all, and especially the authentic mystics, who practised existentialism; and that atheistic existentialism, in spite of its recent success with the general public, is nothing but an anomaly, one of those absurdities with which, unfortunately, history abounds.

Chapter 4

The Existentialist Tradition and Christian Thought

The controversy about the use of the term ' existentialism '
or ' existentialisms ' seems to me to be somewhat in the
nature of hair-splitting. As I have already said, the suffix
' -ism,' conveying the idea of a system, as applied to the
philosophy of existence, is incompatible with the dynamic,
' open ' character of existence. I grant the followers of
Sartre a monopoly of the word existentialism, although
this would make it difficult to include such an authentic
—even from the Sartre point of view—existentialist as
Sören Kierkegaard, who would not have agreed with any
of the dogmas of *Being and Nothingness*. One thing is
certain, that the phenomenological method and existential
view of the universe cannot become the monopoly of any
one school. I would go so far as to say that those who make
the best use of, or conform most faithfully to the fundamental demands of this method, are not the disciples of
Sartre. Writers such as Camus, Malraux, Romano Guardini,
Karl Barth, Mounier and Berdyaev seem to me to be
incomparably more in tune with the spirit of existential
philosophy than Sartre, Simone de Beauvoir or even
Merleau-Ponty.

The Gospel of Christ

Are we entitled to speak of a ' Christian existentialism '? It obviously depends on what we mean by the words Christian and existentialism. A Christian idealism or a Christian materialism is evidently impossible; and if we take the word existentialism in the doctrinal sense of a particular school, and then put it on the same level as the doctrine of Christianity, we are certainly not entitled to dignify it with the adjective ' Christian.' On the other hand, if we take my conception of existence and of the philosophy of existence, Christian existentialism will rank, in the corpus of Christian philosophy, with, for example, scholasticism or Thomism. These also are more methods than a body of doctrine, since Thomist and existentialist Christians—Jacques Maritain and Gabriel Marcel for instance—believe the same dogmas and profess the same doctrine.

' Christian philosophy '—as the first Christian writers called the Gospel message in its entirety—appears to the historian of ideas as incontestably an existentialist reaction against the often profitless speculations of the Neoplatonists, the Stoics, the teachers of Judaic law. Jesus did not teach a new cosmology, or even a new theology, and we know nothing of his opinions on mathematics or physics, or even if he had any. His mission was to bring men a message of salvation. We should seek in vain in his teaching for any learned speculations on the nature of God, such as those favoured by the Greeks and, later, the Schoolmen. Jesus certainly preached God the Father and the mystery of the Trinity, but this was only because man labouring under the burden of sin needs to know that his relationship with God is not that of a slave to his master, of a criminal to his judge, but that of a prodigal son to an infinitely loving father. He preached the Trinity because this was necessary for man's realization of his destiny and his salvation. ' Be ye perfect as your Father in heaven is perfect.' ' Be ye one as my Father and I are one.' Every religious truth which Jesus taught his disciples was incarnate in his life and work, even before it was expressed in words. No other philosopher or sage embodied to such a degree the direct expression of an authentic existential experience. In Christ existence and existentialism are truly one.

His disciples, fired by their contact with the burning zeal of Christ's human existence, felt themselves called to share his experiences and imitate him. Anyone reading the Gospel carefully for the first time is bound to perceive that Jesus wished at all costs to avoid the danger of his teaching ever being constricted into too narrow and too precise a form, which would no longer be adapted to the speech and ways of thinking of the Palestinian Jews at the time of the Roman occupation. This is why he gave his gospel such a concrete shape, embodying his doctrine in parables and illustrations drawn from the everyday experiences of the people. Long before Bergson and the modern existentialists, he used descriptions and images as more apt than abstract definitions to convey adequately the most profound teachings.

It is enough to compare the Gospel of Christ with, for instance, any of Aristotle's writings in order to realize the very great superiority of the ' existentialist ' method used by Jesus to the deductive and abstract processes of the philosophers. The Jewish rabbis themselves had adopted —whether wittingly or unwittingly matters little—the systems currently used by the Greek sophists of analysing sacred Scripture according to the rules of abstract logic. Any educated man today who is not a professional philosopher, would find it very difficult to follow Aristotle's deductions, strictly logical as they are. These deductions, in fact, are so intimately bound up with the scientific, ethical and religious conceptions of Aristotle's time, that it is practically impossible to take any except a scholarly interest in them. In order to understand any of Aristotle's works we have first of all to acquaint ourselves with the whole body of his philosophic system, and, to a certain extent, with the whole history of his times. The same is roughly true for the exegesis of the Jewish rabbis.

I should not like to claim that an extensive knowledge of the history of the times and of the people of Jesus, and a critical and accurate analysis of the literary styles of the New Testament, would be completely unnecessary for a reader of the Gospel. The work of people like Lagrange, de Grandmaison, Prat and Daniel-Rops have undoubtedly led innumerable readers to seek to know Christ, and in consequence to read his words. Such excellent preparatory study, however, is in no way essential for one who desires to read and meditate on the Gospel with the maximum spiritual benefit. How many, educated and uneducated alike, have never opened a single book on the history or the exegesis of the New Testament, and yet have it as a constant companion, and never have the slightest difficulty in understanding its deepest and most essential meaning? Nor is it necessary to be a great scholar, nor even to believe in the divinity of Christ, to recognize that there is far more depth and mystery in the ' philosophy ' of Jesus than in that of Aristotle.

In the Gospel all is vibrant and concrete. One would seek in vain for even a hint of a scholastic system or technique. It is not necessary to be deeply learned to realize, as we read the Gospel, that the men who recorded the teaching of Christ as shown in his deeds and words, did not intend to write merely history, or even theology. The chronology of the facts interested them but little, and logical definitions even less. They are relating—often, from a strictly literary point of view, very unskilfully—their own existential experience, their encounter with him whom they justly recognized as the son of the living God.

Eulogy of the existentialist character of the Gospel does not, however, imply that this should lead us to reject all formalized doctrine or theological systems. These undoubtedly have their place in the economy of salvation, for man's intellect has also need of evangelization, and can only receive this message through methods adapted to the intellect. Besides, as we saw in the preceding chapter, notional philosophy is useful to existence, since it excludes all sectarianism, even existentialist. All we claim here is that the Gospel itself is not a system in competition with other systems, but the way of salvation, a way which the Master as well as his disciples followed to the end.

Early Christian Writers

The early Christian writers—both the authors of the New Testament narrative and the first Church Fathers— carried on the existential tradition of the Gospels. Even in the first outlines of Christian theology in the Epistles of St Paul it is rare to find logical deductions or *a priori* reasoning, and where the Apostle does resort to these methods it is only to convince those of the Jews and Greeks who were accustomed to such intellectual exercises. Paul's discourse in the Areopagus of Athens is the most characteristic example of his use of a dialectic which is not native to him. As soon, however, as he really speaks direct from his own heart, we can see that the true source of his teaching is his personal experience in Jesus Christ, and that his credo comes not from books but from living experience. All that he did was to give a universal dimension to his personal contact with the risen Christ and, with his powerful intellect, systematize his interior existential experience.

Take, for example, the famous Pauline doctrine, which is the foundation of his whole theology, the doctrine of the Mystical Body. In order to explain his theory to hearers who had been trained in the school of Greek philosophy, the Apostle uses comparisons borrowed from these philosophers or from mythology; but it would be quite wrong to say that it was from these philosophical reflections or from these mythological recollections that he reasoned that all Christians are members of a single body, the Church, whose head is Christ. If Paul is prepared to give his life in witness that Christ and his Church are one, and that every Christian is, in a certain way, a Christ, this is because on the road which leads from Jerusalem to Damascus the crucified Christ appeared to the fanatical Saul, the persecutor of Christians, and asked him: ' Saul, Saul, why persecutest thou Me? ' Here we have what is called the ' existential fact.' the inner experience of Saul-Paul. The second stage of the phenomenological method, as we said, is to reflect on the fact, and this was what Paul did. He had not known Christ during his life on earth, nor had he been one of the crowd who cast stones and demanded that Pilate should crucify him. But he had taken part in the stoning of Stephen, and had actively contributed to the putting to death of many other disciples of Christ, so that he immediately understood the meaning of Jesus' question. He made no protestations of innocence, nor did he exclaim, like the sinners mentioned in the Gospel: ' But Lord, when and where did we persecute thee? ' Later reflection upon his experience on the road to Damascus was enough for him to conceive the doctrine of the Mystical Body. Even the Epistle to the Hebrews itself bears only a superficial resemblance to the casuistry of the rabbis. While it is true that he was obliged to meet the rabbis on their own ground and consequently to resort to the kind of arguments they favoured, we have only to read this Epistle carefully to see that its real doctrines were founded on quite a different basis from the more or less fanciful rabbinical interpretation of Old Testament texts.

When St Paul speaks of Christian joy or Christian suffering, he speaks from his own knowledge, in his body and in his soul, of what it means to suffer for Christ, and because to him it was granted to know while yet on earth the unutterable joy which Christ promised to all those who love and serve him.

The earliest great Christian philosophers and theolgians —Origen and the other Alexandrians, and St Gregory of Nyssa and the Cappadocians—may seem at first sight to have broken with the existential tradition of the New Testament in favour of Greek logic and metaphysics. As they had received their intellectual training in the Greek schools, they naturally used the expository methods which they had imbibed there to translate their Christian ideas. This Hellenism, however, only touched the expression and form of their thinking without affecting the content. A careful examination will reveal the inner pulse of their thought and its origin in the purest Christian experience. The magnificent work achieved by Henri de Lubac and Jean Daniélou in rehabilitating Origen, who was the first and perhaps the greatest creator of systematic Christian doctrine, proves how unjustly this intellectual genius has been accused of Neoplatonism or of Gnosticism, whereas the mainspring of his philosophy was the love which bound him to his Lord. It was only much later, at the time of the great controversies about the nature of God, that Christian philosophy lost its existential character and became, in some cases, a Christian sophistry.

The fact that too many theologians lost sight of the existential character of their faith and were too exclusively influenced by the prestige of the pagan philosophers gave rise to most of the heresies in the Church, from the Gnostics in the second century up to the ' modernists ' in the beginning of the twentieth. As soon as a Christian goes back to the very source of his faith, he becomes ' existential.' This is why all authentic Christian philosophy is, in some degree, existential and Etienne Gilson was probably correct in using the word existentialism in connection with St Thomas Aquinas.

St Augustine

Of all the classical writers, both pagan and Christian, St Augustine is certainly the one whose words reach most directly into the heart and mind of men today. We might say that practically all the well-known writers of antiquity, and even most of those who were popular in the nineteenth and in the beginning of the twentieth centuries cannot now be read without tedium and constraint, whereas, as we have already seen, the works of St Augustine are still, fifteen hundred years later, read with intense interest. Not only the *Confessions*, but also the *City of God*, most of his sermons and even his youthful writings, beginning with the *Soliloquies*, are authentically ' existential ' in the sense in which I have defined the term. It is true that a certain number of the problems which he had to face, and the theories which he refuted, no longer interest us, but the modern student will see them only as the vehicles of Augustine's personal thinking, the vitality of which is still undimmed.

St Augustine's reflections all spring from the intimate experience of man, not of rational man, man ' in-himself,' but man in the concrete, that is to say, profoundly divided, rent by warring appetites and desires. As a Christian, Augustine sees the origin of the fundamental ambiguity of the human reality in original sin. But as the man that Christ came to save is historical man, Augustine speaks with as much, if not more sincerity than modern existentialists concerning the tragic character of the human condition. The soul of man is perpetually torn between a more or less confused feeling of belonging to God and a desire for absolute independence. A being who was created to love God above everything cannot turn away from God without denying his own reality. The tragic condition of man is described by Augustine in his *Sermo* 142, in words which are completely existential:

In departing from itself the soul departs from its Master. By contemplating itself it takes pleasure in itself and is enamoured of itself. But in the same way, it also departs from itself and for this reason lives at present in external dissipation. It loves only the world, and what is perishable and terrestrial. If it loved only itself, denying its Creator, this would already be a crime against its own being, because one degrades oneself by loving the lesser instead of the greater. The soul is indeed less, infinitely less than God, as the creature is inferior to the Creator . . . We should love God so much that, if possible, we forget ourselves . . . The soul forgets itself, but it forgets itself in setting itself to love the world, instead of forgetting itself in love of the Creator of the world. Love of the world chases it out of itself, and by so doing it is lost. It is no longer capable of judging its own acts, and goes so far as to justify its iniquities. It puffs itself up and takes pride in arrogance, in lust, in worldly honours, in possessions and riches, in power and in vanity.

The soul, however, neither can nor will be satisfied in this state of dispersion, tranquilly installed in mediocrity. It suffers from its divorce from God, even if it does not want to admit the real cause of its unhappiness, its feeling of inadaptation and of insecurity in the midst of the world which it has preferred to God. Little by little it ' recognizes its deformity and becomes enamoured of beauty.' (We must remember that Augustine, like all the Church Fathers, had a Platonic education, and still held the perception of beauty as the most important of the means of spiritual elevation. It was only much later that he awarded this primacy to ethics.) Recognizing the ugliness of an existence centred on love of the world and reverting to love of the beautiful, the soul will endeavour to shake off its dissipation and rediscover its original condition of unity and reverence. This ' conversion ' or recovery of the lost unity of his ' self ' is obviously not accomplished without grief and suffering for the sinner. In his *Confessions*, and particularly in Book VIII, Augustine gives a magnificent description of the dramatic return of man to himself and to God. Bitter warfare is raging in the depths of his heart and mind. A perverse will deflects intelligence from truth, and a warped logic offers what is ugly and false to a heart seeking love, in place of what is beautiful and true. Little by little, however, the grace of God regenerates both the will and the intelligence until at last their re-integration is accomplished.

Everyone realizes that St Augustine's philosophy of the human condition, with its dramatic description of man's turning away from God, seduced by the false values of the world, his dissatisfaction and his spiritual suffering in his exile from the Beautiful and the Good, his laborious search for enlightenment and his final return to the house of his Father, was not based upon theoretical speculation on abstract postulates. Augustine, as all existentialists, was not concerned with the construction of a philosophy or a theology whose dialectic would be solely rational. His theology and his philosophy proceed from his own human, empirical experience. He does not, however, shut himself up in narcissist self-contemplation. From his individual experience he is able, thanks to his existential reflection, to distinguish those truths which are of universal application, and here again modern existentialists merely follow in his footsteps.

As Jean Guitton showed at a period when St Augustine was hardly thought of as an existentialist, the saint was the first Christian philosopher who clearly grasped the place of temporality in the fragile and unpredictable existence of man. His experience as a human being and as a priest had taught him that nothing in human existence is definite or stable, that everything in it is in a state of perpetual flux. For existence the present is only a fiction, an idea; only the past and the future have reality. God alone is being; man exists only through his participation in God's being, by virtue of God's presence in him. ' If thou wert not in me, O God, I should not exist. Or rather I ought to say that I should not exist if I were not in thee, for whom all exists, and in whom all exists.' There have been few philosophers who were as acutely conscious as Augustine of the extreme fragility of human reality, which of itself is nothing. Human reality, however, is not nothingness, precisely because the presence of God informs it. Whatever man does, no matter how radical his withdrawal from God, he can never become nothingness, for God's presence in him is unceasing. But in order that man can realize his destiny, achieve the happiness and the peace for which he longs, he must allow a different form of divine presence to take shape in him, not a presence which is imposed and given once and for all, but one freely accepted.

So this preacher of grace who recognizes that all initiative of salvation belongs to God alone, is just as convinced as any modern existentialist of man's liberty. Without this liberty there would be no tragedy in his condition, no greatness or weakness for any of us. True, he argued against Pelagius, who affirmed that man can realize perfection by the strength of his will alone, since Augustine had learnt from his own personal experience that the will, without the grace of God, is little inclined towards the good. But he argued with equal vigour against the Manichean heresy which denied liberty and professed moral determinism; without liberty there is no existence. Man's liberty, however, is not absolute, moreover it is infirm and consequently needs the grace of God to be made whole again and to realize man's supernatural purpose, which transcends the capabilities of human freewill even were this not weakened by sin. Augustine, commenting on St Paul's words, ' I have the will, but not the power to accomplish,' wrote: ' There are some who consider these words as the negation of liberty. But how can one deny this freewill since Paul says, " I have the will "? We can certainly will because we have freewill. That it is not in our power to realize the good, is a consequence of original sin.'

6

Compared with divine eternity, the temporal character of man's condition is certainly imperfect in duration. But it is far from constituting a negativity pure and simple, since time is also the dimension of our spiritual maturity, the factor of our growth. Time consoles us in the midst of our tribulations, heals our spiritual scars, melts away our sorrows. Here, too, liberty must play its part in giving a sense of direction to our immersion in time, and making it a power for diminution or growth.

Unswervingly faithful to the phenomenological method of introspection and reflection on the data supplied by his meditations on his inner self, Augustine elaborated a philosophy of existence which is the same in all essentials as that advanced later by existentialists. His faith enabled him to avoid the descent into absurdity and despair which trapped the atheistic existentialists of the twentieth century; but it is important to note that this faith is not a *deus ex machina*, invented for the good of the cause by a man too cowardly to live the absolute non-sense of the human condition. Neither is it the conclusion of a proposition of formal logic; it is itself a direct existential experience. Among all his spiritual or psychological experiences, his experience of faith was that which most influenced Augustine. It is unfortunate from the point of view of the prestige of existential philosophy that some of the most prominent existentialists did not trouble to study the existential faith of St Augustine. It would have saved them from making so many and such regrettable blunders.

St Bonaventure

Augustine was the last original Christian philosopher until the beginning of the era of mediaeval scholasticism. The Christian writers of the centuries which succeeded

him were essentially faithful to the orientation which
Augustine gave to Christian philosophy. Not until the
twelfth and thirteenth centuries did the phenomenological
method of introspection and existential reflection begin to
give ground to the philosophy of Aristotle.

Several celebrated teachers, however, followed Augustine even in his phenomenological method and his conception of human condition. Prominent amonst these was
St Bonaventure, whose work is more particularly a struggle
against Aristotelian rationalism, which appeared to him to
be absolutely incompatible with the inspiration and
tradition of Christian philosophy. He argued against the
view that autonomous reason could arrive at truth by its
own unaided powers, and found it incomprehensible that
Christian teachers should argue as if faith was non-existent.
For Bonaventure, as for Augustine, faith was not a fact
apart from self, but coincides with its very reality. To
discount faith, even if only for methodological reasons,
seemed to him a wilful mutilation of our power of knowledge, above all of our power to know spiritual realities,
and God in particular. While reason can, it is true, demonstrate the existence of God by rational proof alone, man
aspires, according to St Bonaventure, not to conclude
that God exists, but to see him.

The mission of philosophy, according to Bonaventure,
is not to satisfy our intellectual curiosity, but to show us
the way of salvation. He affirms, even more insistently than
his master Augustine, the existential primacy of the salvation of the soul over theoretical knowledge. Philosophy
for him is wisdom, a wisdom indicating the path leading to
supreme Wisdom, which is God. ' The man who knows
the best way to the summit of Mount Alverno is not the
man who knows by heart all the various paths leading to

the top, but he who chooses one of them and takes it with the firm intention of following it right to its very end.'

Like the existentialists Bonaventure believes that the primordial and most fruitful act of knowledge is introspection, the direct confrontation of the soul with itself. In this way the soul can decipher in its own substance the image imprinted on it by the Creator at the time of its creation. The basis of Bonaventure's philosophy is, in fact, this self-knowledge of the soul. Reason should, naturally, reflect on the immediate facts which the soul discovers in itself, but these reflections must be guided by faith.

Bonaventure repudiates the rationalist theory which makes God an object of human knowledge. Divine enlightenment is that by which we know, it is not an object of knowledge. Love and charity alone can attain to God.

My only reason for not dwelling on the ' existentialism ' of St Bonaventure is that in essentials it is the same as that of St Augustine. Like the latter, Bonaventure has an acute realization of human contingency. But not having been through the same personal experiences as the Bishop of Hippo, he had not the same intense perception of the dramatic character of existence. Yet he is very conscious of the risks and the responsibility of our thinking. It must come to a decision and of necessity choose one or other of the two possible paths: the way of life, or the way of everlasting death.

Blaise Pascal

Whereas the classic scholastics, while preferring rational to existential philosophy, knew how to preserve a middle course and maintain contact with concrete reality and inner experience, their successors of the fourteenth, fifteenth and sixteenth centuries were not equally wise in this. They adopted not only the pedagogic processes of rationalism, but also its postulates. In philosophy as well as in theology, only the rational was acceptable, the ambiguous character of the human condition was not understood, and ' faith ' was taken to mean a purely intellectual allegiance to a body of doctrine which, it is true, claimed to derive from the biblical revelation but insisted primarily on its rational justification. Neither philosophy nor theology concerned themselves with inner experience.

The existentialist tradition of Christian philosophy was, however, preserved by the mystics. The great Rhineland mystics of the fourteenth and fifteenth centuries like Thauler, Eckhart, Suso, and the anonymous author of the *Imitation*, were the spiritual heirs of the tradition of St Augustine. Truth for them was achieved above all by the way of inner contemplation, and reflection must be based not so much on the rules of logic as on spiritual experience. They countered the rationalistic simplification of the theologians by the image of actual man, his struggles and his inner contradictions. Later, the Spanish mystics, following St John of the Cross, conceded the use of the scholastics' terminology, but the content of their philosophy remains existential and their main concern was with genuinely existential problems. Christian existential philosophy had, however, to await the coming of Blaise Pascal to discover a new master, in whom the philosophy of St Augustine was renewed and perfected.

To give a complete account of the existential philosophy of Blaise Pascal, to analyse and comment on the whole body of his philosophical and religious work, would require an entire book, and is impossible within the limits of this chapter. The existential themes of Pascal are not incidental,

but the very heart of his thinking. Pascal was consciously
' existentialist,' although the term itself was first invented
by Sören Kierkegaard two centuries later. Innumerable
books have been devoted to the work of this philosopher
who is considered as the greatest French thinker of all time,
and probably one of the greatest Christian thinkers.
Amongst these Romano Guardini's *Pascal ou le drame de la
conscience chrétienne* (published by Editions du Seuil) seems
to me the best appreciation of the existential character of
Pascal's work.

Few men are as ' complete ' as Blaise Pascal. The image
invented by the Jansenists—a bigot, despising the world
and its pleasures—had no resemblance to the real Pascal.
Scientist, philosopher, man of the world and man of God,
passionately in love with life and love, and yet capable of
renouncing it all for a higher love; possessing an all-
embracing desire for knowledge—such were some of the
facets of his extraordinary personality. His Christian faith
was certainly deep and fervent, but it was a faith which
had been won in bitter struggles. The same ardour which
he evinced in his scientific researches and in his controversies with his many opponents, is manifested in his
philosophic reflections and in his search for God.

As I have already said in a previous chapter, for the
existential philosopher there is no distinction between
philosophy and the act of existing. This is true for St
Augustine, Kierkegaard and the others; and it is even more
true where Pascal is concerned. It is impossible to separate
the incomparable richness of his works from the intensity
and passion of his life. A born scientist, his capacity for
observation far surpasses that of nearly all other existentialists, and his power of reflection was equal to that of the
greatest. We may wonder whether Pascal was ever tempted

to elaborate a philosophical system as did Descartes, Malebranche and Leibnitz. All we know for certain is that the circumstances of his life and the impetuosity of his nature prevented him from ever finishing a single philosophical book. We are almost inclined to be glad of this fact, since the existential character of his work is thus even more perfectly affirmed; Pascal himself never thought of human existence as perfected or final.

A brilliant mathematician, Pascal was well versed in reasoning, and had a wonderful grasp of the processes of abstract logic. As soon, however, as he began to reflect on human reality and the uniqueness of its place in the universe, he saw that the ' geometrical mind ' was completely incapable of comprehending why man is man. It is fortunate that man is not restricted to the ' geometrical mind,' but still has intuitive sensitivity. Otherwise we should have to content ourselves with the Cartesian concept of man which is purely objective and scientific, and reduces man to animal and animal to machine. Just as the ' spirit of geometry ' has reason for its ' organ,' so intuitive sensitivity also has its organ, which is the heart. Pascal's conception of the ' heart,' which holds such an important place in his philosophy, is not derived from simple emotion or sense impressions. It is founded on spiritual experience, and it foreshadows the ' intuition ' of Bergson, or the ' knowledge through homogeneity ' of Maurice Blondel. The ' heart ' enables us to appreciate the reality of the inner life, with all its richness, whereas the ' spirit of geometry ' can give us only an abstract knowledge. Love—for the idea of ' heart ' implies the presence of love—far from deluding the mind, makes it only more lucid and more penetrating. Pascal's own abundant spiritual experience taught him how false was the contemporary idea that only a cold, objective intelligence, devoid of all affections, could find truth. He knew that only intelligence allied to passion was enabled to transcend appearances, and to penetrate reality in all its complexity.

Existence, said Pascal, does not progress clearly and regularly like a proposition in logic. It is made up of contradictions, tensions and conflict. This he knew full well from his own personal experience. All through his life Pascal was torn by various passions and tensions, even his spiritual life was filled with conflict and anguish. The existential anguish which, since the time of Kierkegaard, has played such an important part in the philosophy of existence, was well known to Pascal, who bore its scars deep in his soul, and had learnt that it is only through such anguish that man comes to break away from the everyday routine of complacent mediocrity to aspire to the beautiful and noble. Existence does not mean and should never mean repose. Leaving a given state of tension behind us, we reach not a state of repose, but a further period of instability and uncertainty.

For Pascal as for all the existentialists, the essence of man's greatness is in his intrinsic consciousness. ' The greatness of man consists in being aware of his insignficance. A tree does not know that it is insignificant.' Even Sartre, with all his instinct for the abject and contemptible, never succeeded in painting a more impressive picture of human wretchedness and baseness than that found in Pascal's writings. Pascal had truly no illusions about humanity. He knew all its weaknesses, and considered man more pitiable and more powerless than the animals. But what Sartre took as the consummation of existential experience, was only a first stepping-stone in Pascal's dialectic. Having described the wretchedness, suffering and terror of man's condition, Pascal does not stop there, he pursues his investigation; and it is thus that he reveals man's greatness, which consists in his capacity for thought, his spiritual being. ' Man is but a reed, the weakest thing in nature, but he is a thinking reed. . . . Should the universe annihilate him, man would still be the greater, because man dying knows himself to be dying, but the universe has the mastery and knows it not.' No matter how extreme the wretchedness of man, it is the ' wretchedness of a dispossessed king.' It is because man is conscious and free, and notwithstanding commits evil and lives in ignorance, that his wretchedness is incomparably greater than that of other beings; but his consciousness and his freedom enable him to transcend his wretchedness and to realize his greatness. His wretchedness thus results from his greatness, and his greatness from his wretchedness. We thus see that Pascal does not gloss over the essential ambiguity of existence.

Unable to bear his state of anguish, man endeavours to escape from it by resorting to ' diversions,' a complex word with several connotations, like all Pascal's terms. We should take it as meaning all acts and words tending to evasion of the real problems of existence. But such diversions are only a pseudo-remedy; and man soon perceives that there is only one way of putting an end to his wretchedness and aspiration towards greatness, by transcending self. He is confronted with two alternatives, either to live above self, or beneath. Here we see revealed the whole tragedy of the human condition, which cannot remain itself. Either it ascends spiritually, or else it falls into the worst kinds of baseness. The reality of sin, on which Pascal meditated so often, explains the fundamental disequilibrium of the human condition. Without sin this condition would perhaps

be dramatic, but not tragic. Reason, a function of the
' geometric spirit,' is obviously incapable of finding itself
among such great complexities. The intuitive sensitivity
and the ' heart ' alone can grasp all this multiplicity and
discover its unity. The heart is not afraid of paradox, since
' paradox is the passion of thought, and the thinker without
paradox is like a lover without passion, mediocre.'

Man's existence is in movement, like a never-ending
stream. ' There is nothing more unbearable for man than
to be in a state of complete repose, without passions,
business, diversions or application. It is then that he realizes
his nothingness, his abandonment, his insufficiency, his
dependence, his powerlessness, his emptiness.' But on
entering the stream of life, not only does he put an end to
his nothingness, abandonment and so on, but he gains
access to a higher existence. Pascal, like St Augustine, held
it as evident that man cannot be realized except in God
alone. The God whom he discovers in the depths of his
soul is, to quote his celebrated formula, the ' God of
Abraham, God of Isaac, God of Jacob, God of Jesus Christ,
not that of philosophers and scientists.' This means above
all that God, for Pascal, is not the conclusion of a logical
argument, but God as revealed by Holy Scripture, who is
present in the heart of man. Not by the use of the traditional
' five ways ' did Pascal discover God, but by his own
spiritual experience. As a believer and a mystic he still
retained the love of the concrete and factual, which char-
acterizes his work as a scientist, and even more his philosophical reflections.

Pascal was, as much as and even more than Kierkegaard,
hostile to all relativity, and liked to scandalize the Pharisees
of his day by his preaching of the Absolute. From this
originated his celebrated controversies with the Jesuits.

The casuistry of the moralists was indeed completely intolerable to him, since it objectified the human act, and consequently God. The Christian should not calculate and count to discover the degrees of mortal sin. He must accept the risks of his faith and give himself to God without counting the cost. Pascal's famous theory of the wager, which has so often been misunderstood, is actually very close to the Kierkegaard conception of risk.

If Pascal's influence on Christian philosophy was not as great as it deserved to be, the reason is mainly to be found in his relations with the Jansenists, and the way in which they involved him in their trivialities. It has taken two centuries to reveal fully the true grandeur of Pascal as a man and as a thinker; and it is to him that contemporary Christian philosophy is indebted for a large share of its vitality.

Chapter 5

Some Contemporary Christian Existentialist Philosophers

It would be impossible to include in this essay, which does not aim at being more than an introduction, even a short list of the names of all the Christian philosophers, since the time of Pascal, who continued the tradition of existential philosophy. With the exception of some Thomists, who are more or less disciples of Jacques Maritain, every Christian thinker whose fame reaches beyond his own circle, belongs to the tradition of concrete philosophy made illustrious by Augustine, Pascal, Kierkegaard and others. This is true not only in France, but in Germany, Italy and Belgium as well; and it applies not only to Catholics, but to Protestants and to intellectuals not belonging to any particular sect. I can consequently mention here only those of the ' Christian existentialists ' who have had the greatest influence on contemporary Christian thought, or who made a genuinely original contribution to it. Even so, I may have omitted some who should have been included.

Bergson and Blondel

Emmanuel Mounier, in his picture of the ' Existentialist Tree,' includes in the branches several philosophers and writers of varying degrees of importance who, without being technically philosophers of existence, played a great part in creating the climate of opinion which fostered the birth of existential philosophy. Thanks to these precursors, the message of the new philosophy fell on already fertile ground.

Henri Bergson was the writer who did more than any other to expose the superficiality of the dogmas of positivist intellectualism. He laid stress on the irreducible phenomena of life and consciousness and enlisted the aid of modern biological science to establish the autonomy of the mind and its predominance over matter. In order to appreciate the true value of the revolutionary character of Bergson's work, one would need a detailed picture of the whole intellectual, and particularly the academic climate of the early years of the present century. Nowadays a ' vital ' philosophy seems very limited to us. Yet how would it have been possible to conceive of a philosophy of liberty and of inner life without first severing the pseudo-unity of the real and the knowable? Once the genius of Bergson had demonstrated the specific character of human reality and the impossibility of reducing it to empiricism, the assertion of existential values was unlikely to meet with serious opposition.

It is not surprising, therefore, that those Christians who realized the extent of the disastrous breach between the edifice of modern thought and the Christian revelation greeted the teachings of Bergson with enthusiasm, and became his warmest adherents. Here I have in mind more particularly Charles Péguy, but also philosophers like Jacques Chevalier and Père Sertillanges, who did so much to undermine the strongholds of the rationalist serenity of the Christian conscience, and forced men to re-examine the genuineness of their faith, and to reconsider what they had falsely assumed to be revealed truth.

Maurice Blondel, whose interests were far removed from those of Bergson, had a similar and complementary influence on contemporary Christian philosophy. Essentially Catholic, he began by a direct study of Christian problems, and in so doing pioneered new approaches to theological research. All the best theologians of this century have been his disciples, directly or indirectly.

His philosophy is not, in the strict sense of the term, any more existential than was Bergson's. Yet if we look more closely, we can see that from the time of the publication of *Action* in 1893 his conceptions were basically identical with those of St Augustine and Pascal. His analyses, more ontological than phenomenological, led him to realize the limits of human nature and also man's unconscious expectation of the grace which would enable him to achieve the goal towards which all his aspirations yearn, but which he is unable to achieve alone. In Blondel's philosophy, the supernatural order and divine revelation, without being, strictly speaking, *required* by nature—nature not being able to demand anything which is not natural— are still however not external and accidental, since they respond to the most ardent wishes of nature. It is the specific fragility of man not to have a natural perfection, and Blondel is quite prepared to agree with Pascal that man is the weakest of reeds and more wretched than the animals or plants, since the latter in order to realize themselves have only to be themselves. Man, however, can only realize himself by escaping from himself, or, as the modern existentialists would say, by transcending himself. But in accepting this surpassing of self he attains a higher reality, and thus establishes his greatness and uniqueness over all the beings of the universe.

Blondel's affirmation of the temporal and spatial reality of man, however, is unequalled. It is in time that man realizes his eternal destiny; it is in the world that he finds the nourishment necessary for the growth of body and soul. But above all it is man who, by introducing mind into the universe, confers on it a purpose and a significance which it would not otherwise have had. ' Matter is for and through life; life is for and through mind; mind is for and through God.' Here we finish with the idea of an opaque and impenetrable universe. Matter is no longer a senseless substance.

The method which Blondel used to construct his system has been called by one of his most brilliant disciples, Père Auguste Valensin, ' meta-psychological analysis.' Our philosopher, particularly in his earlier works, quite deliberately abandons the processes of deductive syllogism, and creates a concrete dialectic which is based on the data of inner experience and the facts of consciousness. He does not, however, confine himself to a simple phenomenology of action, to which Blondel gives a very broad definition, including external and creative action as well as psychological activity. Therefore, those Catholics who criticized his teaching when his first *Action* was published showed a misunderstanding of his method. Blondel reveals ' being,' or, if you prefer, essence, beneath the phenomena, and reflection on this being leads him to the affirmation of the absolute Being which is also pure Action and pure Thought. He thus opened the way which all those who aspire to the construction of an existential ontology and metaphysics must necessarily follow.

Blondel's dialectic reveals the utter insufficiency of human reality and of all that is created, the basic instability of our existence, torn between higher and lower, the weak-

nesses of our consciousness. This is not to deduce its
absurdity, but to put us on our guard against pride and
superficiality, to prepare us to receive the mystery and
abundance which is offered to us from above. ' Tragic
optimism ' was practised by Blondel even before Mounier
invented the term.

Deeply conscious of the originality of human freedom
(which he does not equate with freewill), Blondel sees the
drama of human existence as a series of choices, of alternatives. These are made in and by time, and yet they reach
beyond time, since neither death nor eternal life are for
man inevitable arising from determinism, but are the
conquests of his free action. Here we see how love takes
its place in Blondel's dialectic.

If Maurice Blondel's philosophy was of an apologetic
character from the start, which drew down on him simul-
taneously the wrath of the university and the distrust of
certain Catholics who were incapable of seeing beyond their
routine, this again was the consequence of his existential
attitude. His intense and out-going spiritual life could
not remain apart from his concrete thought, so immersed
in the whole of reality.

Blondel always refused to be considered an existentialist,
firstly because he considers existentialists as deniers of
reason, whereas in his view only rationalism itself was to
be condemned, and to demand reason is just as legitimate
as, for example, to demand ' heart.' As we have seen, I am
in complete agreement with him on this point. He also
criticizes existentialists for affirming an existence without
essence, though the latter alone can give the former con-
sistency and meaning. But we have already seen that now
the best existential philosophers, even amongst non-
Christians, no longer reject essence; and consequently

Blondel is nearer to us today than he himself realized. His nearness to existential philosophers is due, above all, to his obsession with the elucidation of the meaning and purpose of existence, rather than to his method; and he prepared Christian thinkers to understand the existential problem.

Karl Jaspers, the Philosopher of Transcendence

Those who favour simple classifications—which often tend to be over-simple—see in Heidegger the master-mind of atheistic existentialism, and in his compatriot, the German philosopher Karl Jaspers, the model of Christian existentialism. In actual fact, Jaspers, who is indeed one of the greatest contemporary masters of existential philosophy, is neither Catholic nor even Christian. A Protestant by upbringing, he considers philosophy to be incompatible with religion. He agrees essentially with Hegel's criticisms of religion, and considers it as a lower stage of intellectual development, the higher stage, naturally, being that of philosophy. Man turns to religion only to escape the anguish of his consciousness which has realized the inherent contingency of existence.

Nevertheless, despite his negative criticism of religion, it is true to say that Jaspers has had a profound influence on nearly all the Christian existentialist philosophers of our time. It is not so much that they approve of his contention that the great mass of humanity cannot live without religion, and that it would be dangerous to liberate them prematurely from the yoke of traditional beliefs. No ' existentialist ' Christian would accept this infra-existential conception of religion. If religion was not the way *par excellence* to existential authenticity, it would have no value in our eyes. But we feel a kinship with Jaspers because he, of all the moderns, has best understood the primordial place which, in a philosophy of existence that is not pure negation, belongs to the idea of Transcendence. It is because existence leads to Transcendence, that it is possible to rise above the nihilism which is the inevitable consequence of the existentialist philosophy of Heidegger or Sartre, that our possibilities of accomplishment become unlimited and, in consequence, that failure and death have not the last word.

Jaspers calls this Transcendence ' Being,' the One, and even God. This does not mean, however, the God of the Christian revelation, a personal Being, since Jaspers blames Christianity for having made the Absolute objective, a God for Everyman, whereas the true God can only be *my* God, who cannot be communicated to another, and has no connection with another's God. Even mystical experience, which is on a higher plane than everyday religion, will not lead to the authentic Transcendence, since it also conceives a God separated from the world, whereas Jaspers' philosophy places Transcendence in the heart of immanence, and he does not believe that God could live and act otherwise than hidden in the world. We should, however, be mistaken in deducing from this that Jaspers is a pantheist. ' We must not consider Transcendence,' he writes, ' as an individual God, separated from the world, nor say that all is transcendent and that God is the all-containing being.' As for atheism, Jaspers repudiates it as pure error, since it results in the denial of all Transcendence and consequently of existence itself.

While it is simple to gather from Jaspers' writings what Transcendence is not, it is quite another matter to find out what it is. In fact Jaspers' thinking on this point, as in his previous description of existence, seems extremely confused.

Jaspers, rejecting all definitions, revelations or similar concepts, sees Transcendence as the unattainable goal of indefinable thought and desire. The dialectical method is unable to lead us to the presence of God; it can only result in our conviction of our fundamental insufficiency, our radical failure, for which Transcendence must compensate. If, however, not even the existential dialectic can unite me to the Absolute, if 'what I learn is always *in* the Whole, but never *the* Whole,' is not this Absolute, this All, a pure chimera, a worse snare than all the consolations of the most static and unauthentic of religions? This is not Jasper's philosophy. For him, the affirmation of Transcendence is a sort of primordial act of existence, a fundamental intuition which needs no proof. ' Existence is either in relationship with Transcendence or it is not.' Or again: ' Existence is nothing else but the search for Transcendence.'

This Transcendence, the object of the ' philosophic faith,' ' is the Other, completely different, not comparable with anything whatsoever.' Jaspers uses terms which many Catholic mystics—of whose works he seems to know very little—would not disavow. Transcendence is the Separate, the absolute One, the sovereign Freedom which is opposed to my freedom. But this Transcendence, for him, is so far separate from existence—although, I repeat, it is not conceivable without existence—that it neither speaks to it, solicits it, nor hears any of its prayers, and is thus more distant from existence than even Jehovah in traditional Judaism. The practical conclusion which results from this, is that his relationship with Transcendence cannot prevent man, as an empiric reality, from ending in failure and thus, in a certain sense, Jaspers' existentialism is just as pessimistic as that of Heidegger.

Jaspers recognizes implicitly, however, that for man

there is another level besides the empirical, and it is on this level that the proper action of Transcendence takes place. Mind exists only because of its élan, its reaching towards the Absolute; and existence can be authentic, that is to say, intense and profound, only through its relationship with the Absolute. It follows consequently that all human moral effort should tend towards this relationship. Aesthetic contemplation and speculative research can help us here. But, once again, it is not Transcendence itself which we can reach in and by our moral effort, but uniquely the relationship with it, which in no way dispenses us from the obligation of remaining faithful to the Absolute. Jaspers admits that such a unilateral fidelity cannot be easy; and he goes on from this to exhort us to courage even in the midst of the despair which is engendered by the inevitable failure of our empirical ego. ' It is enough for me that the being of the One exists. My own being, which perishes entirely as *Dasein*, is indifferent, provided that I continue to aspire as long as I live. In the world there is no true consolation which can make intelligible and bearable to me the mortality of all things and of myself. But in place of consolation there is the consciousness of being in the certainty of the One.' Such a philosophic creed is near to the mysticism of Nietzsche, for whom Jaspers always had an admiration.

Transcendence presents itself purely and simply to consciousness. ' It presents itself to me as the *reality without possibility*, as absolute reality, beyond which there is nothing. I am silent before it.' All man's freewill is nothing but an aspiring towards Transcendence; and since I have no existence except through freewill, I consequently exist only as an aspiration towards Transcendence. Jaspers' doctrine of the ' cipher ' is extraordinarily profound, and from some points of view recalls the symbolism of St Bonaventure, with this difference however that for the latter the model of all symbols, God, can himself be known through revelation and, in a certain manner, even by philosophic reason, whereas the model of the cipher, Transcendence, is completely outside our grasp, and the cipher teaches us nothing about its own ' nature.' ' The cipher is, for existential consciousness, the only form in which Transcendence appears—a sign that Transcendence remains for existence, hidden, it is true, but does not disappear.' The whole *Dasein*—the world, nature, man as an empirical being, the firmament and history—can become a cipher, and ceases by this fact alone from being a simple empiric reality. In other words, reference to Transcendence confers a meaning and a dignity on all things which saves them from the final defeat. By means of these realities as ciphers the Absolute makes itself known to men; and it is thus that on the basis of experiences which are empirical and deceptive in themselves, that the metaphysical experience takes place, which consists in deciphering Transcendence in all its finite realities.

In spite of the low esteem with which he regards religion, Jaspers does not completely condemn it. This is because religion itself, considered as mythologies, miracles and images of the supernatural world, becomes a cipher of Transcendence. The same is true of intellectual speculation. All things in the world, becoming ciphers, cease to be opaque and become transparent. God is thus infinitely distant in himself, but can become near in the cipher. Since ' there is nothing which cannot be a cipher,' God is thus manifest everywhere. Even death itself, although a supreme defeat on the empiric level, can become a cipher of Transcendence, and thus ceases to be a fatality in order to become an act of freewill.

However confused Jaspers' ideas about Transcendence and its cipher, the final result of his philosophy is not, however, nihilism, as is that of Heidegger and Sartre, but a luminous hope. Philosophic faith, which he considers as the allegiance of freewill itself to Transcendence, enables him to affirm that empirical, perishable reality is not the only reality, and that, in consequence, failure will not have the last word. It will not, therefore, surprise us that Jaspers should be considered by the generality of Christian existential philosophers as one of their own. It is true that he seriously misunderstood the real essence of religion and presented an easy target to those Christians who will have nothing to do with existential philosophy. But he comprehended, better than any other non-Christian existentialist, the metaphysical link between existence and Transcendence; and his Christian disciples had no difficulty in differentiating between what is truly valuable in his philosophy and what is only due to a more or less incidental misunderstanding of religious reality.

Max Scheler

For some time another German, Max Scheler, had at least as much influence on Christian philosophy as Jaspers. This was particularly true in France and in other Latin countries.

Scheler adopted Husserl's phenomenological method, as did Jaspers, but he was more successful in avoiding any philosophic dogmatism and his thinking is explicitly spiritual in the Christian meaning of the term, in spite of his leanings towards a certain pantheism at the end of his life. Scheler took human emotions as what one might call the raw material of his existential research. Analysing suffering and grief, resentment and forgiveness, repentance and love, he finds something very different from a more or less irritating organic disability from which man should free himself in order to become a free being. He discovers that all emotion is directed towards an object and is intentional, as, according to all the existentialists, is existence. The object towards which all our emotions tend has always an existential value; and it is this value which confers a purpose and a meaning to our emotions and makes them into human acts. For example, there is nothing more legitimate, on the empirical level, than the struggle against suffering. Yet, from the point of view of Scheler, should we not rejoice that science has not yet succeeded in abolishing all suffering? In his very beautiful book, *The Nature of Suffering*, Scheler reveals the purifying and spiritualizing forces which are hidden beneath suffering. The same is true for repentance, which in itself is never pleasant, and which yet, in certain cases, results in a magnificent existential vindication.

Without in any way weakening the intimate solidarity which links man to the world, Max Scheler's great merit was to emphasize, at a time when the contrary view was affirmed as a scientific dogma, the profound originality of man's situation in the world (this is actually the title of one of his best books). His analyses come to the conclusion that it is mind which differentiates man from the empirical world. The ' essence ' of the mind consists in liberty and in the consciousness of self, so that it is only in beings who manifest in themselves the presence of these two ' faculties ' that we can speak of mind. These are known by language, moral conscience, religion, science, and the feeling of kinship, which so far, in our universe, have been found in man alone.

Louis Lavelle

Louis Lavelle is certainly not the best-known of contemporary philosophers; but he is incontestably the thinker who has had the greatest academic influence in France. More of a 'sage' than a man involved in the controversies of his day, he was not a popular figure to the general public, not even to the more educated section. On the other hand, the profundity, the extreme honesty of his thinking, the elegance of his style gained him the sympathy, esteem and admiration of professional philosophers; and it is through them that his teaching, or rather his wisdom, will long be disseminated.

It was thanks to his collection *Philosophie de l'Esprit* that the educated French public learnt of existentialist philosophy in other countries. Kierkegaard, Berdyaev and Scheler were introduced to France in this way. As for his own work, it is probably, with that of Maurice Blondel, the most complete 'summa' of Christian philosophy in the twentieth century. The problems which engage him are more or less the same as those which occupied Jaspers and Scheler, and he also uses the phenomenological method of introspection and analysis with the most rewarding results. Unlike too many French philosophers during the last seventy-five years, who had great difficulty in shaking off the terminology and concepts of their German masters, and consequently felt obliged to invent new words which were completely foreign to the spirit of the French language, Lavelle always deemed it incumbent on him to express his thoughts in elegant and clear French. It would be well if all those who have really something to say, would take him as their example instead of being incomprehensible.

Lavelle, like Scheler, sees mind as the distinguishing characteristic and patent of nobility of human reality. His

love of clarity prevents him, however, from falling into
the snares of the pantheism to which the German philosopher succumbed. It is true that the divine penetrates
created matter through the mind; but mind will never
be a strictly individual property of man; it is a participation
in the Absolute which communicates with itself and communicates being.

For Lavelle as for Jaspers' human existence is to be
conceived only as a function of Transcendence. He does
not see the latter, however, as an absolute Other which
does not communicate itself and which is unknowable;
it is the personal God who loves, and whose love confers
on existence its purpose and significance. The underlying
optimism of Lavelle's philosophy is consequently more
justifiable than that of Jaspers, who demands it in the name
of a faith which can only be philosophic.

I have called Lavelle a sage, because his philosophy,
while it does not ignore all that is moving and ambiguous
in the world and particularly in human existence, yet
possesses a serenity, and exudes a peacefulness which
clearly distinguishes it from existentialism, even Christian
existentialism, in the proper sense of the term. While it is
true that three of his more readily comprehensible books:
L'Erreur de Narcisse Le Mal et la Souffrance and *La
Conscience de Soi*, deal with the most contingent and the
most ambiguous aspects of the human condition, we realize
that his dialectic is derived from such an elevated source,
from the Absolute itself, that there is no room in his
philosophy for doubt and anguish.

Gabriel Marcel or Neosocratic Existentialism

For the general educated public (in France and even
beyond its borders) the Christian existentialist *par excellence*

is Gabriel Marcel, so much so in fact that many people think of Christian existentialist philosophy only along the lines laid down by Marcel. When the followers of Sartre seek to ' prove ' that Christian existentialism is impossible, they aim at the weaker points of Gabriel Marcel's philosophy.

This evidently does too much honour to Gabriel Marcel, though he is actually a profound and influential existential philosopher. No other modern thinker, as far as I know, has carried phenomenological analysis as far as he has done in his famous *Journal Métaphysique* the title of which alone is enough to indicate its topicality and his desire to reach beyond the phenomenal world; a task which his later works have continued. His own conversion to Catholicism should be considered as the concrete result of the first period of his philosophic meditation, for philosopher and philosophy are united in him as in no other contemporary writer. Although Marcel turns to the theatre to give concrete expression to his metaphysical thinking, we should seek in vain in his personality for the exhibitionism which Sartre, for instance, never quite succeeds in losing, even in *Being and Nothingness*. If, however, we compare him with Claudel, or to take the case of another philosopher, Jacques Maritain, whose own conversion resulted in a tranquil possession of truth, we see that Gabriel Marcel, since he became a Christian, has never ceased to be anxious, to interrogate himself about the content and the forms of his faith, to seek with anguish the purpose and the significance of human existence in time. He can never be satisfied with an objective pseudo-certainty; he demands his own personal certainty. There is consequently nothing more untrue than a statement by a journalist that Gabriel Marcel, since his conversion to Christianity, was no longer an existentialist. It would perhaps be more correct to say that it is since his conversion that he has become one. This explains why, in spite of the excessive austerity of his analyses and the eremetic quality of his style, he appeals so strongly to his contemporaries who, anxious and unsatisfied, fasten avidly on a philosophy in which they hope to find, not an answer to their questions, but an indication of the direction in which they should pursue their own search for truth and enlightenment.

To enable us to appreciate the cardinal principle and originality of Gabriel Marcel's contribution to twentieth-century Christian philosophy, let us deal for a moment with his now famous distinction between problem and mystery. It is, in fact, undeniable that the faith of very many Christians was troubled and often destroyed during the centuries of triumphant rationalism, because the mysteries of religion did not lend themselves to solutions such as science brought to the problems of the empirical world. After the time of Descartes, the French more especially recognized only a single way of knowledge, that of the experimental sciences. Everything which did not comply with these laws was considered as unreal and absurd. They even went so far as to demand that God should come and perform his miracles before the Academy of Sciences before they would believe in him!

Gabriel Marcel, who first learnt philosophy in the school of rationalist idealism, found his metaphysical reflections coming up against a wall of interdictions. It was then that he intuitively discovered the distinction between the mysterious and the problematical, and that he was enabled to unmask the sophistry of the scientists' claims. 'A problem,' he writes in *Being and Having*, 'is something I meet, which blocks my path. It confronts me, whole and entire. Mystery, on the contrary, is something in which I find myself involved, and consequently consists essentially in that which is not whole and entire before me.' A problem is capable of solution and the sphere of the natural coincides with that of the problematical. It is a very dangerous temptation to convert the mystery into a problem, for that would lead one to seek for a solution of the insoluble. A mystery can certainly be explored; but this exploration belongs not to the sphere of reason, but of existence. We may even say that it is mystery which illuminates the sphere of existence.

All the principal existential realities, and not revealed truths only, are mysteries and not problems. When someone like Sartre commits such enormities as the reduction of love to hate, of faith to deception, it is because he began by converting the mysterious into the problematical. Gabriel Marcel's acute and luminous analyses of faith, hope and love; of fidelity, suffering, joy and liberty, bear witness to the philosopher's scrupulous care in respecting the intrinsic nature of mystery. In the *Journal Métaphysique* and especially in *Du Refus à l'Invocation* the philosopher places the phenomenology of being on a solid basis, which one would seek in vain in the descriptions of the human condition by Jaspers, Heidegger and Sartre. In *Homo Viator* he analyses with his customary precision the mysteries of family and paternity. Finally, in *Les Hommes contre l'Humain*, a book which is one of the easier for the ordinary reader, but also in some respects the most controversial of his works, he describes the situation of man in the modern world.

Although Gabriel Marcel is without equal in the domain of phenomenological analysis, he is more aware than any other philosopher of the basic insufficiency of a phenomenology as such. Because it is accepted by existentialists like Heidegger and Sartre, is the reason why Marcel refuses to be classed as an existentialist. Man for him, as much as and even more than for Jaspers, is only man when he transcends himself, becoming more than man. It was not by chance that Gabriel Marcel's first philosophic work was called *Journal Métaphysique*, since he is firmly persuaded that all philosophy which does not culminate in an ontology and a metaphysic, is not even entitled to be called philosophy, and has no *raison d'être*. But his is a concrete ontology, his metaphysics is an existentialist metaphysics.

In the two volumes of *Mystère de l'Etre* Gabriel Marcel demonstrates his mastery of his method, and proves that an existential metaphysics is not an absurd dream. In future no one can claim, without blatant bad faith and crass ignorance, that there is an irreducible opposition between being and existence. Ontology and phenomenology are two successive stages of the same action of the mind in its search for truth. ' Existence,' he writes, ' presents itself in reality as implying and also surpassing everything to which they tried to reduce it . . . The more my existence affects an *inclusive* character, the more the interval which separates it from being, tends to shrink, in other terms the more I am. This is as much as to say that one cannot in any way conceive being as severed from existence.' It is clear that Gabriel Marcel does not content himself, in such a serious matter, with gratuitous statements. The passage cited above comes as the conclusion of a strict existential analysis. Marcel, indeed, can never be criticized for a lack of precision in his analyses. If most of his books discourage a reader uninitiated in the mysteries of phenomenology and metaphysics, it is because his analyses are generally so exhaustive that the reader becomes involved in the labyrinths, and loses sight of the main idea. Gabriel Marcel's philosophic investigations proceed in a convoluted manner, and one needs to be very familiar with his work to appreciate its exceptional scope, especially as the philosopher seems incapable, and probably unwilling, to turn his philosophy, into a system—for, like all genuine existentialists, he detests systems—or even into a doctrine. He leaves it to others to benefit from his intuitions and his analyses to form a more synthesized impression of the mysteries of existence. Personally, I have often found Marcel's analyses to be a starting-point, almost a ' generator ' and guide to my own reflections on existence.

In the same way as Jaspers—by whom he was apparently greatly influenced in his first contacts with existential research—Gabriel Marcel sees the need of Transcendence at the root of existence. This need is not simply a need to surpass, since all surpassing is not necessarily an act of Transcendence. It is need for absolute Transcendence. ' The need for Transcendence,' he writes in the first volume of *Mystère de l'Etre* ' shows itself primarily . . . is felt primarily as insufficiency.' Insufficiency, however, does not imply aspiration towards Transcendence. There are insufficiencies which are strictly material or temporal, whereas the idea of Transcendence implies a complete surpassing of these.

In Gabriel Marcel's view, however, the Transcendence towards which existence aspires is not the inacessible and ineffable absolute which, as we have seen, Jaspers considers it. ' There must however be an experience of the transcendent as such, and the term has no meaning except on this condition.' Here I am in complete agreement with Marcel, and consider this as a magnificent extension of Jaspers' intuition, the extent of which the German philosopher was not capable of appreciating.

In order to conceive of and undertake such an experience one must first free oneself from any restricting prejudice about the notion of experience. The ideas of an artist or a mystic are just as valid as those of a chemist or a physicist. 'Experience infinitely surpasses the domain of our senses.' Gabriel Marcel writes in the same book, 'and it is equally manifest in what we call the inner life.' Jaspers did not understand this, and it is for this reason that his Transcendence remains confused, and that he felt obliged to oppose it absolutely to the God of religion.

That Transcendence which Gabriel Marcel reveals as the deepest need of existence is called God. He is not the God of the philosophers, whose privileges were asserted by Jaspers against Pascal, but indeed the God of Abraham, Isaac and Jacob, the God of Jesus Christ. We may even say that the main victory of Gabriel Marcel's concrete ontology and existential philosophy was to have put an end to the traditional opposition, which dated from Pascal, between the philosophers' God and the God of religion. His analyses of faith, begun in *Being and Having* and concluded in *Le Mystère de l'Etre*, his analyses of freewill and grace, of death and existence after sin, are the finest landmarks in the authentically Christian existential philosophy.

Nicholas Berdyaev

The Russian philosopher Nicholas Berdyaev was very different from and yet had much in common with Gabriel Marcel. His books have for the most part been translated into French, and were an important factor in the propagation of Christian existentialism.

From the point of view of methodology, Berdyaev is incomparably less faithful than Jaspers and more faithful

than Gabriel Marcel to Husserl's phenomenology. A
mystic intuition, nearly related to that of Bergson, is,
according to him, the most adapted to reach the spiritual
world, mediating a knowledge—imperfect, it is true—of
the mystery of man and of God. His thinking is mainly
based on a spiritual experience and in this regard he should
be classed among Christian existentialist philosophers. His
faith does not forsake reason, but transfigures it, becomes
its inner light, and thus confers on it the power to understand liberty, the source of being and of creation, and all
the other existential realities. For him metaphysics and
mysticism are the two supreme forms of philosophic
knowledge.

Being Russian, Berdyaev had less need to form his philosophy of existence in opposition to rationalism and idealism
than those of us who are from the West. It is true that in
his youth he was a Marxist, but in the Russian manner,
that is to say, more interested in mysticism than in dialectical materialism. It is, in fact, a characteristic of the Russian
genius to learn from the West, but to assimilate Western
teaching in a fundamentally different fashion.

In the case of Berdyaev, before his philosophy encountered Western existentialism, and adopted certain elements
from it, it had already found its own form. His masters
were more particularly Dostoievsky, Soloviev, and to a
certain extent, Tolstoy, and through them all the Russian
intellectual philosophy. In this he found the remains of the
old Gnosticism of Greek Christianity of the early centuries,
which harmonized so well with his own mystical but
anti-dogmatic spirit. It is not surprising, therefore, that
when he came into contact with Western philosophy, he
was very little influenced by Husserl and Jaspers, but became an enthusiastic disciple of the more or less pantheist

German mystics like the Catholic Eckhart, the Protestant Jacob Böhme, and that strange figure, Franz von Baader, who, in the eighteenth and nineteenth centuries, attempted a singular reconciliation between Catholicism and a half-German, half-Gnostic mysticism. Berdyaev was attracted only to free minds, with a mystical tendency, and he himself figured as a ' heretic ' in his own Orthodox Church.

The purpose of life and the destiny of historic man were the two main preoccuaptions of Nicholas Berdyaev's philosophy. In his eyes the great enemy of existential authenticity was the objectification of man and mind, and even of God, which modern science as much as traditional philosophy had been guilty of. To assert the rights of the person, a unique aim justly avoiding all objectification, was the main task of his philosophic campaign. It was because Marxist Communism which was in power in his homeland subordinated the concrete individual to the social abstract, and personal destiny to collective history, that he went into exile and was one of the first to denounce, in his *Problem of Communism* the spiritual perils of that doctrine. This obviously did not prevent him from denouncing with just as much vigour the materialism of a West worshipping at the altar of Mammon.

The starting point of his philosophy is neither God nor man, but God-man; his philosophy is consequently neither a theology nor a humanism, but a ' theandry.' The Christian mystery of the Incarnation is the central event of human history, and it is only on this basis that one can understand man and his history, God and his works. From Berdyaev's point of view, there is no human, existential problem which is not spiritual, and everything spiritual necessarily passes through God-man. To seek elsewhere than in Christ the solution (or ' comprehension,' as Gabriel

8

Marcel puts it) of such important problems of existence as human liberty, for example, is to depart from the path of truth. The Incarnation, the Redemption, the Trinity, Original Sin, the Eucharist—Berdyaev does not deny any of these, but he interprets them in a disconcerting manner.

Man, for him, is nothing apart from God. How absurd it is to discuss the alleged antinomy between human liberty and divine prescience, since man derives his liberty from and in co-operation with God, which does not prevent him from being truly free and acting authentically. ' It is not only man who acts, but God also, it is not only God, but also man.'

The antithesis of Berdyaev's dialectic is that of nature and mind, which means the antithesis between necessity and liberty, or again between the thing and life, the existential world and the objective world. To understand the history of man, it is not enough to learn it. I must live it in myself, in depth. Even economic life itself cannot be understood apart from the spiritual.

Berdyaev was one of the first existential philosophers to underline the social character of existence. Always taking his stand on his basic theandric conception, he refuses any man the right to think of his individual salvation without at the same time thinking of the salvation of all his fellow men. His *New Middle Ages* and his works on Communism are as much an integral part of his metaphysics as, for example, his *The Destiny of Man* and *Freedom and the Spirit*.

Emmanuel Mounier and Personalism

In his *Arbre Existentialiste* Mounier himself includes personalism as one of the branches of modern existentialism, although the fight for the rights and dignity of the person played an infinitely greater part in his life than research into the purpose and meaning of existence. But the one presupposes the other, and it is incontestable that the human person for which Mounier fought during the whole of his short but ardent life, was not an abstract entity but a concrete existent. His *Traité du Caractère* as well as the innumerable articles in the review *Esprit* which have been collected in several volumes, reveal a philosophy of existence which takes its place in the long tradition of Christian philosophy whose history we have traced here.

The two philosophers who, directly or indirectly, most profoundly influenced personalism were Gabriel Marcel and Nicholas Berdyaev. From the point of view of political temperament, and even of temperament alone, Marcel is the complete opposite of Emmanuel Mounier, who was the herald of the emancipation of the poor and the uncontested leader of a numerous team of young intellectuals, who were all far from sharing his Christian beliefs. It was, however, as a disciple of Gabriel Marcel that Mounier realized more and more the irreducible character of the human act and understood the dignity of the person, which one is not entitled to sacrifice to any temporal end. He also derives from Marcel the profound unease which never allowed him to rest on the ready-made, in the certainty of a tranquil possession of his sociological position as well as his Christian faith. During the twenty years of my acquaintance with Mounier, I never saw him engage in the ' dialectic of having.' Being, existential being, was his main pre-occupation.

As for Nicholas Berdyaev, Mounier, especially during his youth, had a profound admiration for him. The two men had the same keen sense of the involvement of the spiritual in the temporal history of humanity, and the same horror of a disembodied intellectualism which took no account of the economic and political realities of the human condition, or compromised itself with outworn forms of civilization.

As a controversial philosopher Mounier took little interest in the Gnostic speculations of Berdyaev on situated freewill or metaphysical sin; but he felt himself responsible, as much as did Berdyaev, for the sins of the world, particularly the sins of the Christian world. The starting-point of the personalist philosophy is the awakening of consciousness to a crisis in civilization, a civilization which calls itself Christian, but which has dishonoured all the intrinsic values of Christianity. Civilization, for him, is something other than a certain amount of material and cultural benefits put at the disposal of a given social group. ' A civilization is above all,' he writes in the *Manifeste au Service du Personnalisme* ' a metaphysical answer to a metaphysical appeal, an adventure of eternal nature, which challenges every man in his solitary choice and responsibility.'

The person must be distinguished from the individual, personalism from individualism. The individual is opposed to others, and individualism claims the autonomy of man with regard to other men, the community of men, and God. The person, on the other hand, is ' the invisible centre to which all is attached '; it is ' the unique cipher ' which would be a ' presence in myself'; it is generosity, and therefore it gives itself and gives. It alone is open to others, to the world and to God; if individuals can constitute only states, persons alone can create communities, since, as Paul Ricoeur rightly says in an essay which appeared in the special number of *Esprit* devoted to Emmanuel Mounier, ' the generosity of the person has as a paradigm the theological virtue of charity, and the mutuality of persons has the communion of saints.' Our civilization is in a state of crisis, because it is depersonalized, because it is no longer based on a community of persons but simply a collection of individuals. As man cannot save himself alone, it is consequently not so much the realization of personal existence which personalism proposes as the influencing of history by the power of thought, so as to create a new civilization. The ' revolution ' that Mounier advocates, must be personalist and communal, as the title of one of his first books indicates.

Personalism thus appears, at any rate in its original form, less as a philosophy than as a pedagogy. It is a moral requirement in view of the personalization of existence. The elucidation of meanings is less important than the promotion of action. Mounier, however, does not ignore the fundamental themes of existential philosophy. He knows that there can be no personal life without solitude, meditation, privacy, respect for the uniqueness of every existent. He has no illusions about man, especially the depersonalized man of bourgeois civilization; and his conception of existence is at least as tragic as that of Sartre. But his philosophy is inspired by a singularly vivacious Christian hope, by the robust optimism which exudes from his whole being, and is not pessimism but, he as says himself, a ' tragic optimism.' His small book *L'Affrontement Chrétien*, which was written in particularly dramatic circumstances during the German occupation, is the most beautiful expression of this tragic optimism. Mounier has no tenderness for the emasculated and saccharine Christianity of this decline of bourgeois civilization; but never for an instant does he doubt the vitality of the Gospel life-force, and beyond the serious crises he sees not the death but the renaissance of Christianity.

As man is at present the slave of the depersonalizing

forces of a dying civilization, the struggle for freedom is identical with the struggle for the personalization of exist-ence. Mounier is very much aware of the ambiguous character of human liberty, and does not let himself be drawn into the snare of vain speculations about freewill or the liberalism in the capitalist régime. ' We are only free,' he writes, ' in so far as we are not completely free,' since personalist freedom is not the arbitrary and so-called absolute freedom of the individual, but is accomplished within the community. It is not freely given, but is the fruit of conquest and entails responsibility. ' My freedom is not just, free-flowing, it is regulated, or, better still, summoned.' Contrary to Sartre, Mounier does not make of freedom the being of the person; but considers it as ' the manner in which the person is all that it is, and is it more fully than by necessity.' Just as the person itself is not being (God alone is being), but ' the movement towards being, and is only consistent in the being at which it aims.'

Chapter 6

Transcending the Common Round

Now that we have seen how far-reaching and continuous is the tradition of Christian existential philosophy, it is time to enquire how this philosophy accords with our lives in the twentieth century, and how it can help us to *exist*. If existential philosophy were only a theory about existence, it would be of but little interest at a time when man feels himself more than ever 'cast into the world,' dislocated and disconnected. But, as I have already said, philosophy, in my view, cannot be separated from existence itself.

Existence is liberty and a perpetual becoming; it is not something ready-made, capable of being possessed. But just because it is liberty, it cannot be determined, since our phenomenological analysis leads us to the conclusion that, contrary to the view of Sartre, man is not *condemned* to be free, but is called to become free. Consequently, he is not condemned to existence either. We know that many people never make any use of the power of liberation which we all receive, at the same time as being, in the form of a potential, or to use the Gospel word, a talent, waiting to be developed. There are many men not only in primitive communities, but also in the most advanced societies, who are untouched by conscience and unmoved by any impulse of liberty. Even among the most civilized and highly-educated there are some who never feel any misgivings, have no ambitions beyond the daily round, never set themselves any problems and see no mystery in anything. They are quite content to be born, to eat and drink, have children and work, functioning as naturally as the animals. Lacking even a relative contact with the Transcendent, they have no existence in the philosophical and spiritual sense of the word, and consequently do not fulfil their destiny as men. Our materialistic civilization has considerably increased the number of these ' inauthentics ' among the educated and privileged in the so-called upper classes.

The first act of existence seems to be anxiety, an anxiety which should not be confused with that apprehension or fear of the immediate future which is often felt by even the most ordinary of men. We shall probably do better, adhering to Kierkegaard's terminology, to call this anxiety ' anguish,' although nowadays the latter word can also lead to regrettable confusion, since psycho-analysts use it in a rather different sense. It is also true that existential anguish sometimes has a psycho-pathological character, as, for example, in the case of Kierkegaard himself. In existential dialectic, however, anguish, together with passion, is the main motive power. Anguish attacks the spurious security in which, knowingly or unknowingly, the inauthentic wraps himself. It makes us re-assess our situation in the world and think about ourselves; it enables us to see the necessity and the possibility of existential Transcendence.

Existential anguish immediately follows man's realization of his basic ambiguity, of the fact that he is never completely that which he is, that he is an extraordinary mixture of finite and infinite, of time and eternity, of determinism and liberty. Kierkegaard rightly saw that were man not a sinner, he would not know the meaning of anguish. It is indeed sin which has destroyed the unity of being, and has created a rift in the depths of our spiritual self. Were it not for sin, we should be existents from birth, and our lives would be a harmonious development of this existence. It is because the war against sin is the main element in our human vocation, that we have no right to content ourselves with an inauthentic conventionalism and that, instead of suppressing our anguish, we should make use of it in the dramatic fight which constitutes existence.

As soon as man wakes from his pre-existential slumber, he realizes that he is, as the Bible says, flesh and spirit, that he is attracted and at the same time repelled by evil, that he is similarly attracted by good, but discouraged by the effort and renunciation required to follow it. This is what was meant by that great existentialist St Paul when he said that he did not do the good which he loved and committed the evil which he hated. Anguish is the consequence of this struggle between contradictory and mutually exclusive realities. We need not think, either, that opting for one or the other of these realities will put an end to our anguish. If we yield to the temptation of evil, anguish-hesitation is replaced by anguish-remorse. If we follow the good, the call of a new and higher good gives rise to a new anguish. The saints themselves were not free from anguish, but were torn by a higher anguish, more like the divine anguish of Christ in the Garden of Gethsemani. Anguish, as a dialectical force, is intended to make us aspire towards the re-establishment of that unity of our self which sin has destroyed, and by this to make us pass from inauthentic routine to authentic existence.

It follows that we should not want to abolish or suppress the anguish which has been awakened in us by the realization of our ambiguous situation in the world. Some, in order to escape from its clutches, take refuge in what Pascal calls ' diversions.' They try to persuade themselves that the daily round is enough for them, that they experience no need, no anxiety which would oblige them to leave the state of comfortable mediocrity in which they have settled themselves, that they expect nothing from life except a little pleasure and material satisfaction. The most frequent result of such suppressed anguish is a neurosis, that is to say, an anguish which is no longer dialectic, but which has become a sheer destructive force.

Existential anguish, according to Kierkegaard, should lead us through three stages: aesthetic, ethical and religious. From the moment when man appreciates beauty, he makes the first breach in the emprisoning wall of the everyday. Love of the beautiful should normally lead man towards love of the good and this will only be perfected when it brings us into contact with God. Unfortunately this norm is not always realized. There are people for whom the aesthetic is the supreme value, and for whom it takes the place of God himself, thus becoming an idolatry. There is also the moralizing bigot, or even the naturally moral man, who feels no need for the absolute, and has no sense of beauty. Neither of these is authentic. Even the religious man himself is not truly authentic, unless he is not only a man who loves the good, as would be expected, but also a man who appreciates everything beautiful and great. A saint like St Francis of Assisi is a striking example of ' existential sanctity.'

We should, however, be mistaken in thinking that the only purpose of existential anguish is to serve as a dialectic for our personal betterment. Sin not only destroyed the inner unity of man; it also brought confusion into the world, and particularly into the community of mankind. Social inequalities—poverty alongside luxury, the exploitation of man by man, war between nations and classes—all these are just as inauthentic, just as contrary to the divine plan as laziness, ignorance and the refusal to evolve in the individual. The existent is not entitled to escape from ' this wicked world ' by taking refuge in the peaceful garden of his carefully cultivated inner life. He should follow the example of Christ, who not only preached the Kingdom of God and prayed in the desert, but also healed the bodily infirmities of men, and laid down the duty of the rich to the poor and the poor to the rich. The parables of Lazarus, of the Good Samaritan, the Beatitude for those who hunger and thirst after righteousness, are an integral part of the Gospel.

The authentic existent should consequently accept his station in the world courageously, and acknowledge his solidarity with his fellowmen. He must not stand aside from the struggles and battles for a better world. There is nothing more illogical than a Christian defender of the ' Establishment,' since no order established here on earth can be the Kingdom of God, the perfect brotherhood of man. Our existential anguish should feed on the injustices and wretchedness which stigmatize human society, and should place us in the vanguard of the forces working to destroy all that is inauthentic, and all that bears the sign of sin.

The fact of deciding to join the attackers will not in itself put an end to our anguish. The active Christian is inevitably placed in a difficult situation by the conflict between his insistence on the purity of his weapons and the harsh necessities of battle. We cannot deny that, in the world today, the communists are the most efficient antagonists of the established order, and we join with them in condemning it as evil and hostile to existential authenticity. We cannot avoid meeting them in the course of our struggle, and we are often tempted to combine our forces with theirs in order to achieve greater effectiveness. The important thing, however, is not only to destroy what is imperfect, but to replace it by something more authentic. Now we know that the communist universe is worse than the disorder against which we fight, since in return for a promised temporal well-being it requires the sacrifice of all personal existential values, whether of liberty, self-intimacy, or the transcendent relation with God, without which there can be no authentic existence. This impossibility of choosing between capitalist disorder and anti-human communist order is the source of the deep existential anguish of a writer like Emmanuel Mounier. The true solution for a really existential anguish is not to resign ourselves to established injustice, nor to submit to the robot rule of Communism, but to find an original solution which would conform to the commands of Christ the victor over sin.

Anguish, as we have seen, confronts man with the need to make a choice. If he refuses, such a refusal is a choice in itself, but a choice which, instead of dialectical and existential anguish produces a short-circuit, a neurotic anguish.

The first choice facing any one who accepts the need to rise above inauthentic routine and to aspire to authentic existence, is the supreme choice which will give a consistent orientation to the existent, and in the light of which all other choices will be made. When I say ' first,' I obviously mean it not in a temporal but in a metaphysical sense, since we frequently make many specific decisions before the absolute choice. We cannot revoke a genuinely absolute choice with impunity, because such a choice engages our destiny both temporal and eternal. That such a choice involves grave risks is certain, and this is why many hesitate before making it. And yet, as long as man has not made his absolute choice, and has not committed himself irrevocably, he will have no means of concentrating his scattered forces and energies on a central axis and will consequently not be able to aspire to a true existential authenticity. There are, besides, some existential values which can only be chosen absolutely. This is primarily true of religion, used in the highest sense of the word, namely, the link which unites man to God. It is not possible to be half-Christian, to pick and choose amongst the teachings of Christ. We cannot, for example, take literally the words of the Lord: ' The poor you have always with you,' and describe as Oriental exaggeration his other saying: ' It is easier for a camel to pass through the eye of a needle than for a rich man to enter the Kingdom of God.' It is because the Christianity of middle-class society refused to make the absolute choice and became relativist that, little by little, it was abandoned by the intellectuals as well as by the masses. It is very significant that, at the beginning of this century in France, the most outstanding conversions to Catholicism were influenced by a man like Léon Bloy, who, from some points of view, was so disagreeable and unjust, but to whom one cannot deny his title of *Pélérin de l'Absolu* (Pilgrim of the Absolute). ' Many strange, deplorable and blameworthy things have been said about Christianity,' wrote Kierkegaard, ' but the most stupid thing ever said was that it was true up to a certain point.' Either it is true or it is false; but it cannot be either one or the other except absolutely. St John, in the *Apocalypse* said the same when he wrote that God requires us to be ' hot ' or ' cold,' but, if we are ' tepid,' he will spew us from his mouth.

A question which sometimes complicates the absolute choice which every authentic existent must make, is the difficulty in recognizing the real Absolute. It is not unusual for a man to take as absolute his country, the proletarian revolution, art, or even another human being. By making these his absolute choice, he turns them into idols, and he himself becomes an idolator. Even religion can become an idol, if it is not understood in the sense of the transcendental relationship of man with God but becomes sectarianism. Sectarianism breeds intolerance, fanaticism, the Spanish Inquisition and the guillotines of 1791. I am, however, convinced that from the point of view of authenticity, the absolute choice of a relative value, in spite of all the pitfalls it holds and all the evils it may cause, is better than a relative choice of the real Absolute. Kierkegaard himself said that he would rather be a highway robber, a seducer or a blasphemer, than a mediocre and respectable man. A criminal, or a sincere and zealous atheist, is in fact not far from being converted to the real Absolute (which does not mean that such conversion would be inevitable, or that the way to conversion lies along these lines), whereas mediocre respectability is never converted. We should not forget that the fanatical persecutor Saul became the great Apostle Paul, whereas Pontius Pilate, the sceptic, who washed his hands in token of a despicable ' innocence,' ended his days in wretchedness.

After the absolute choice comes another choice which I call the ' relatively absolute.' This relates firstly to the choice which we should make of ourselves. We must *consent* to our concrete self, even if it appears to us as incomparably less attractive than our idealized image. Obviously we should not compromise with mediocrity. But in order to construct something really lasting, we must build not on shifting sand but on solid rock. In order to become what we should be and desire to be, we must first accept ourselves as we are, with our real qualities and defects. The hysteric who deceives himself first, and then deceives others, can never become truly creative.

The second act of the ' relatively absolute ' choice will concern our concrete ideal and fundamental project. Values such as the choice of a calling, profession, way of life (marriage, celibacy, priesthood, monasticism, etc.), love, friendship, and so on depend on this choice. The obligations consequent thereon are important. Yet death dissolves marriage, the Pope can dispense from religious vows and reduce a priest to a layman, and, in theory at any rate, a change of vocation or of profession is always possible.

As for the purely relative choices, they are generally contingent on our fundamental project, and their values depend on it.

According to its importance, every choice involves a promise to God, to ourselves or to others. Each act of choice in fact implies an obligation of fidelity to the chosen value. All engagements are binding, but it is the nature of the choice which determines the durability of the contract. If I have chosen God and the exclusive service of God by baptism or ordination, no person or thing can terminate my commitment. On the other hand, my engagements to my fellowmen, or to society in general, can be broken if the reasons are sufficiently grave. When we come to a more or less provisional engagement, such as keeping an appointment or accepting an invitation, it is allowable to break it if my reasons for doing so are proportionate to its importance. The authentic existent, however, never commits himself lightly, and consequently he will never break a promise, even an unimportant one, without very good reason. It is, in fact, essential that promises should be respected, if human society is to become a brotherhood and not an abyss of mistrust. It is equally necessary, if the self is to be reunited into a harmonious whole.

All engagements and loyalties, it is true, involve the renunciation of values, sometimes very important to us, which are incompatible with the nature of our choice. If I choose the married state, I cannot live monastically. If I join a revolutionary movement, I shall no longer be able to live in peace and comfort. If I take one woman for a wife, I shall be obliged to renounce all others. The choice of one profession normally precludes another. The ambition of a Gide to possess all, sample all and pluck every flower, obviously cannot be reconciled with commitment and loyalty. But he who does not make his decision, will never be other than a dilettante, an ' aesthete,' and will never attain authentic existence. Commitment and loyalty, although involving renunciation and sacrifice, lead not to an impoverished but to an enriched existence. All the great existents were men and women who were deeply committed, superlatively faithful to their fundamental project, whether it was an apostolate, politics, a military career or an intellectual, artistic or scientific profession.

Commitment and loyalty to a person or a cause do not in any way compel us to be fanatics, or to reject everything outside the object of our commitment and loyalty. I am a Catholic and a Christian, but my loyalty to Christ and the Church does not at all oblige me to close my eyes and my heart to all the authentically religious and spiritual life in other creeds. The fact of loving my homeland does not in any way require me to show a chauvinist contempt for foreign countries. Even faithfulness to one's own wife does not involve being blind to the beauty, the charms and the tenderness of other women. Fanaticism has never been a sign of authenticity in commitment and loyalty. On the contrary, depth psychology generally reveals serious hesitations and weaknesses in the faith of intolerant and fanatical bigots. The most chauvinist nationalists are nearly always those whose patriotic conscience is far from pure, and who, instead of putting themselves generously at their country's service, have used it for selfish ends. When a man shows particular jealousy of his wife, it is a sign that his love is no longer sincere. Only the man who is completely dedicated to a person or cause, can understand that others may make a choice which is diametrically opposed to his. Christ's absolute loyalty to his Father was far from preventing his profound love for his apostles, his friends in Bethany, all the men of his own time, and those still unborn. It is generally those married men who are most authentically faithful to the sacrament of marriage, who can show the greatest delicacy and even gallantry to other women.

A more profound objection to our viewpoint is that shown in the attitude of those who object to any definite commitment—whether it concerns the indissolubility of marriage or of religious vows—and to any promise of loyalty, who deny that it is metaphysically possible for man to commit himself or be faithful. If in fact existence is only a succession of phenomena and psychological states, if what I am today has no ontological relation with the man who will bear my name tomorrow, in a month or in some years' time, if ' I ' is only a grammatical fiction, then obviously no commitment is possible, any oath of allegiance would be an absurdity. How could I commit another, or ask another to keep my promises? And as there can be no authentic existence without a choice which commits or without loyalty (Sartre's choice involves one in nothing, and is purely gratuitous), we must logically conclude in the inevitable bankruptcy of all existence.

If, on the other hand, I believe authentic existence possible, if I accept choice, commitment and loyalty as existential values, it is because I am firmly convinced, after a closely-reasoned existential analysis, that existence is not only a whirlwind of phenomena blown up by some capricious force, but the realization of an *essence*, of my essence. The ' I ' is not a simple grammatical fiction; it expresses an ontological reality. In spite of all physical and psychical changes which have taken place, I am the same man today as the man who, twenty years ago, took a certain path, swore loyalty to a certain person, and this person to whom I gave my loyalty is also still the same being.

Many of our contemporaries are afraid of a choice involving a commitment and implying loyalty, because they fear it will involve their giving up one of the values which today is highly esteemed, that is, disengagement. Always to be able to get away, to be ever responsive to new experiences, never to refuse any possibility, this philosophy of complete disengagement, which is expressed by Gide's Menalcus in *Les Nourritures Terrestres* is, or rather was before the last war, the ideal of many men and women of this century, however few have been able to put it into practice. Disengagement being synonymous with simple and passive expectation, is obviously irreconcilable with commitment or loyalty, and must avoid all relationship with the Absolute.

There is a grievous error at the root of this conception of disengagement. True disengagement derives not from the spirit of possession, but from poverty. If we consider the world and our fellowmen as belonging to us, or revolving around us, we can obviously not commit ourselves and still keep our disengagement. Actually, I should never try to possess others. Even my own person does not belong to me, and I am not the centre of my universe. It is I, rather, who belong to the rest of the world. I am certainly access-ible to the summons of the Absolute, but not passively. God, the world, and my fellowmen do not demand that I should suffer them passively—commitment and loyalty would effectively oppose themselves to such disengagement —but they expect from me exactly that creative initiative, free choice, commitment and loyalty, which are so difficult. Only the truly disengaged person, that is to say one who is not encumbered with self, is capable of this self-forget-fulness, this subordination of his own interest to the com-mon good and to the whole, of this detachment from what he has and what he is, all of which are indispensable to a truly existential commitment, to a loyalty which is not mere routine. And it is because existence cannot attain its fullness by a single and unique choice, by a single and unique commitment, that, in all our choices and commit-ments, we must always remain open to other choices and to other commitments. The absolute choice, the irrevocable commitment in the service of the Absolute, do not destroy our disengagement, but they direct it, and draw it up from that state of mere passiveness which it would otherwise have.

It is by remaining disengaged that the man who is committed and loyal avoids becoming sectarian, fanatical and narrow-minded. He has, of course, and must have his own ideas, convictions and ideals, and is true to them. But he must not forget that no human mind can simul-taneously encompass all truths. However intelligent we are, there are always, in total truth, aspects which we have still to understand. It is consequently worth while to listen to others, to put ourselves in their place, and allow them to teach us. No confusion or ambiguity can be caused by such humility.

True disengagement is not easy, and can only be achieved by hard struggle. Our egocentricity, a consequence of sin, makes us eager for possession; deceptions and failures may make us sceptical, and cause us to close our minds to those appeals and solicitations which urge us to re-examine our postulates.

If we could commit ourselves in complete awareness, if we were able to know all the results of our choice in advance, probably no one would refuse to choose, and the heavy obligations of loyalty would intimidate us less. But it is impossible to calculate exactly all the consequences of our choices, promises and commitments. How many unknown factors there are in joining a political party, getting married, or entering the priesthood or monastic life! The young man may desire to serve God as a priest. How could he foresee that one day he would have superiors who did not understand him, or a ministry which did not in any way correspond to his ardent hopes? Another man falls in love and marries. How could he imagine that after a few years the charming girl would turn into an intolerable shrew, or that their children would be sickly, or that his earnings would not be enough to allow the family to live in reasonable comfort? And this is the case for all choices and existential commitments, which all involve an enormous element of risk. We can never even be completely certain of having found our vocation and of being able truly to realize it. And Catholic theology, condemning the Calvinist theory of predestined salvation, teaches us that we are never completely certain of our eternal salvation. Even there the element of risk remains.

It is because our destiny must realize itself in time, and that temporal duration is not a smooth mechanical development but intermittent creation, that our existence, no matter how we view it, is always vulnerable. The creative act is indeed inherently unpredictable and not susceptible of scientific control. Nothing in our existence is laid down; we must make our own destiny. In any case, risk is implicit in the theory of man's liberty. We can speak of chance, of the ' law of life ' where an animal or any other being in nature is concerned. They realize their destiny equally well in death or natural decline, or else by becoming the prey of the hunter or by being garnered by man. If man was pure liberty, absolute master of his destiny, he would not be exposed to risk, because for God there are no risks.

The more authentic the existence the greater the risk, that is to say, the proportion of personal liberty is greater. Even were it possible to abolish all risk, any man who desires to live intensely has not the right to do so, since this would inevitably result in a deplorable relapse into the inauthentic. That the French youth of the inter-war generation showed so little taste for risk, was a grave indication of the ageing of the race, since a people whose youth confine their ambitions to the civil service or to cashing dividends, is a people who are condemned by history. Since the war, fortunately, there has been a renaissance of the love of risk and of adventure. Never have there been so many dangerous explorations of virgin forests, inaccessible peaks, polar regions and deserts. This is a good sign in itself; but we must agree that for some people adventure does not represent an answer to a call or a vocation. It is nothing more than an escape from reality, a sign of a lack of courage to face the real risks of existence. We should not, in fact, confuse a desire for existential risk with foolhardiness. There is an immense qualitative difference between the man who risks his life for a scientific project, to defend an ideal, or to save a drowning man, and the man who risks his life in bravado by throwing himself into a swirling torrent or a street thronged with traffic. As liberty is not an end in itself, so risk has no existential significance unless it is devoted to authentic progress. He who loves risk, however, even useless risk, and has the necessary will-power, has more chance of becoming an authentic than the man who is obsessed by a desire for security at all costs.

The existential Christian does not look to his religion to provide a consolation, an escape-route, or more success in commerce. He does not believe that it is enough to wear this or that scapular, or recite this or that prayer, to be ' assured ' of salvation. As a disciple of Christ, he knows that he exposes himself to the risk of persecution, that it is not always the good who are the most favoured by ' destiny '; and he does not forget, either, that the Kingdom of God was promised only to those who take it by storm. It is because the sole religion he knew was the ' insurance ' type, that Nietzsche spoke with so much contempt of Christianity. ' There are many things which disgust me in your good men,' he said. ' I wish they could be set on fire by some mortal folly. This folly should be called Truth, Loyalty, or Justice. But their virtue consists in living a long life in a pitiable self-content.'

The acceptance of existential risk is often folly; but it is also the only way for man to emerge from his egoism and from his small and narrow narcissist universe. It puts an end to the spirit of possession, to the false security of inauthentic routine, and demands that we should live in readiness and hope. How wearisome and lacking in tragic intensity would be the life of one who was granted the power to foretell his fate. Knowing ourselves exposed to risk, we put our trust not in ourselves but in God, hoping that he will stretch out his helping hand to free us from snares. It is evidently not in passive waiting, but in courageous and confident advance, that we expose ourselves to risk.

The existence of the inauthentic is characterized by its lack of fire and purpose. Everything in it is ' reasonable ' and calculated. He distrusts any passion which could upset the ' order ' which he thinks he has created in his life. A marriage or a career entered into for its material prospects, a religion ' conforming to the requirements of reason,' which is to say, devoid of the folly of the Cross and of ' excessive ' generosity—this is the ideal of the respectable bourgeois. Some of Paul Bourget's novels provide the finest examples of this kind of ' wise ' and ' reasonable ' life, but one which is also inevitably and repellantly commonplace.

Our analyses and historical examples combine to prove that the only authentic existence is one which is passionately lived. The man who sees things and people, himself and others, only coldly and objectively, will probably never be able to make a choice, or take a decision which would commit him to a definite and dangerous loyalty. Our reasons for not getting inovlved, for not taking risks, will always prevail, theoretically and practically, over those calling for a leap into the unknown of existential becoming. If the young do choose the risks implied in marriage and parenthood, they are not guided by ' reason ' (reason, says Bergson, always advises the egotistical good of the individual), but are swept away on the tide of strong passion, namely, love. A soldier would never volunteer for a danger-

ous mission on the dictates of reason alone, since his life
is his dearest possession. He is urged by another passion,
namely, patriotism. There are always more reasons for
keeping one's money than for giving it to the poor, for
leading a quiet and uneventful life than for devoting
oneself to scientific research or the exploration of undis-
covered lands. It was Pascal who said that there could be
no human greatness without passions; and it is more
particularly such violent passions as love and ambition
which the Christian philosopher praised.

Passions should not of course be deified. Passions, as
we all know, can destroy, create disorder, and lead to
anarchy, as the novels of Dostoievsky or Balzac show. But
if we recall the appalling disasters caused by such master-
pieces of reason as the discoveries of science, we may not
indeed absolve crimes of passion, but put them in their
proper perspective. Neither reason nor passion is good or
evil in itself. It is the use which is made of them which
justifies or condemns them. It would be absurd to blame
reason, as do some irrational philosophers and artists,
because of its abuses or exaggerated cult. It would be just
as wrong to outlaw passions because of all the murders and
adulteries called ' crimes passionnels.' What would become
of the Passion of Christ, since not cold calculation but
passionate love for man led the Son of God to accept
incarnation and death on the cross?

The opposition of passion to reason is actually quite
mistaken; and it is because of this separation and opposition
that throughout history the one and the other have been
responsible for more evil than good. It is not true that
nobler men are guided by reason alone, and that dynamic
passion prevails only in more common minds. St Paul, that
zealous persecutor; passionate lovers such as Mary Mag-

dalene or St Augustine; ambitious men like Ignatius of Loyola and Charles de Foucauld—all became passionate apostles. However, in order that neither reason nor passion should become destructive, they must not cancel out one another, but harmonize. To become creative, reason must be passionate (as great scientists and thinkers are passionate for knowledge) just as passion needs to be guided by the light of reason.

'In a great soul all is great.' 'A stormy life is attractive to great minds, but gives no pleasure to the mediocre,' writes Pascal in the *Discours sur les passions de l'âme*. In fact, the more authentic and spiritualized an existence is, the more passionate and impassioned it is. It is obvious that the sub-men of Sartre and Gide are not capable of loving like the heroes of Dostoievsky. As we saw previously, with Kierkegaard, the worst evil which can befall an existent is the loss of passion, since it means an irrevocable descent into mediocrity. Even a theologian as convinced of the value of reason as St Thomas Aquinas said that morally it was better to do good with passion than to do good coldly and calculatingly, even when the object of calculation is eternal salvation. How wrong it is, then, as much from the theological point of view as from the point of view of existential authenticity, to say, as some Christians do: 'I have no merit in loving others, because I do it spontaneously,' that is to say, passionately. Passion in itself subtracts nothing from the value of the moral act, and man is just as free and responsible in his passions as in his reason, that is to say, he is never entirely free, which does not prevent him from being so, at least existentially. If in fact passions often prove more dangerous than reason, if they generally destroy more than they create, it is because of the inveterate and tenacious prejudice that education should tend to develop reason and suppress passion. As it is not so easy to vanquish such a powerful force, passion irrupts every now and then into the would-be reasonable order, where it can obviously only wreak destruction. Instead of trying to abolish passions and limit ourselves, in consequence, to a commonplace and colourless life, we should educate ourselves and our children to use this passionate force for good, by putting it at the service of our own vocation and the work of God, which we are called to realize in ourselves and in the world. Passions are like those juvenile delinquents who do wrong only because they have not been taught to do good. No one will deny that there is a risk in refraining from suppressing one's passions. But have we not said that risk is inseparable from any truly authentic existence?

The decisive moment in the fabric of an existence comes when it is seized by a great and powerful passion. It is then that life begins to be worth living, for this great passion will throw a dazzling light on everything which formerly was only obscure and enigmatic. No longer shall we be afraid to commit ourselves, no longer shall we be intimidated by difficulties and risks; rather shall we welcome them. Only the man supported by a strong passion will be capable of unhesitating sacrifice, of becoming an apostle and martyr. It is the quality of passion which sustains us. Although struggling under the load of everyday life, we do not always feel its presence; and it will help us to live intensely even in aridity, isolation and the inevitable monotony of the daily task. We must also remember, as has already been stated countless times, that it is generally the most deeply passionate men who are least liable to the erratic impulses of any one particular passion.

Like Kierkegaard, Jaspers also considered faith as one of the most important existential values. Faith for the former was, it is true, a demanding and tragic Christian faith, whereas the latter emphasized a ' philosophical faith.' The fact remains that existence only has meaning in relation to Transcendence, and only faith can bridge the gulf which separates the two.

The Marxists, the atheistic existentialists, and the disciples of Nietzsche agree in considering belief in God as a sort of cowardice. For the first faith is an escape for those crushed by the struggle for a living, and will necessarily disappear when at last man finds happiness on earth. For the others it is because man is too cowardly to face his absurd and hopeless situation as a being-cast-into-the-world, that he invented God and religion. According to all of these, a man who is strong and courageous, actively committed, should emancipate himself from any faith, even the kind of philosophic faith conceived by Jaspers. The Marxists and the atheistic existentialists alike thus expound their Hegelian analyses of religious alienation. None of them troubled to analyse the phenomenon of religion on the existential level.

We cannot deny that for many men today there is no longer any mystery or any religious problem. It is certain too that such men, whose minds and deeds are unenlightened by faith, are not necessarily all mediocre, that there are many among them who live intensely, and whose existence seems to bear all the signs of authenticity. It is equally irrefutable that many of those who do profess to believe in religion, live exactly like the unbelievers; and their faith does not seem to play any part in the choice of their vocation, their intellectual or political allegiances. If there were no believers except such as these, there would obviously be no point in a chapter on existential authenticity in speaking about belief in God.

We should however be bad phenomenologists not to realize the existence of another kind of believer whose existence is completely centred on that relation with Transcendence, which is their faith in a unique and living God. These believers are perhaps fewer than the first. Yet they alone can demonstrate the existential scope of faith. There is an old methodological principle that, to pass a worth-while judgment on a given reality, we must know it above all in its purest aspects. If, in order to condemn communism, we limit ourselves to the most dishonest and mediocre representatives of this ideology, how shall we understand its political successes, and the attraction which it has for so many sincere and intelligent men? It would be easy for us to refute atheism, if only criminals and those rebelling against poverty were unbelievers. But there are also men like Malraux and Camus, who do not believe in God. In the same way, to understand the existential extent of religious belief, we must observe it first of all in those who live it most authentically, whose existence would be incomprehensible without the ' faith factor.'

The complete believer is, of course, the saint, and above all, as Bergson so well said, the model and the source of all sanctity, the God-man, Jesus of Nazareth. The Gospel will be a dead letter for any one who reads it, and ignores the bond which united Jesus to his Father. Such amazing lives as those of St Paul, St Augustine, St Francis of Assisi, Theresa of Avila, Père de Foucauld, and others, would seem an incomprehensible folly if we did not realize that their faith in God and in Jesus Christ was their centre and magnetic pole. And we do not need to go to these celebrated and, for most of us, inaccessible, saints to understand existential faith. What honest and unprejudiced man can say that he has never met a man, a woman, girl or young man, whose existence was beautiful, and intensely beautiful because completely dependent on Christ? They are to be found in all surroundings, in all classes.

For authentic believers, faith is not superimposed on their already naturally-constituted existence. It illuminates and guides not only the spectacular and heroic deeds of the great saints, but also the humble and daily actions of some mother of a family or some poor peasant. It is true that faith draws them into relation with Transcendence; but Transcendence is no longer for them the inaccessible Absolute. It is God calling and helping them. Religion, for these Christians, is not an insurance against the risks of existence, neither is it a simple philosophy giving satisfying and ready-made answers to all the problems and questions which confront man. Religion is existence itself. Far from eliminating risk, it is religion which urges us on to meet these risks, by preventing us from lazily resting on the past. It does not insulate the believer from the world, but gives him a true realization of his responsibilities before history; the efficiency of his temporal action is not lessened, but on the contrary increased by its relationship to the eternal.

The authentic believer will never be self-satisfied. Having chosen life, how can he content himself with what is dead? Neither existential anguish, nor passionate love of life will suffer from faith; rather will they be raised by it to a higher plane. And faith alone can counteract that supreme defeat of all empiric existence, namely, death. The believer does not live in this world as if he was already dead, because he knows that temporal death is not the end of life, but the passage from a necessarily imperfect temporal existence to perfect eternal life. He will not rebel against the inevitability of death, nor will he resign himself to it. He will do all in his power so to intensify existence here on earth that it will give him the necessary impetus to take the great transition through death into eternal life. It is only in the light of faith that the existence of the Christian is founded on a ' tragic optimism.'

Chapter 7

From Solitude to Communion

From the beginning existential philosophy has had to fight against the materialization and over-socialization of life. Accordingly it proclaims that man has a right to solitude. Sometimes, however, as is bound to happen with any vigorous defence against serious danger, the battle has been waged very emotionally and often with a certain amount of exaggeration. Such, for instance, was Kierkegaard's declaration that men should not even seek to associate with one another, because only as an individual has man access to God.

Spiritual and psychological experience undoubtedly confirms that authentic existence is only possible for one who has experienced solitude. The material impossibility of being alone today, and the psychological incapacity of far too many people to appreciate solitude, are undoubtedly the main reason for the lack of authenticity in the modern world. Solitude is necessary so that man may reflect, take stock of himself and of his position in the world, and fit himself to respond to the call of the Absolute. I do not know of any religion or any spiritual philosophy which does not endorse this truth.

Solitude must not, however, be confused with isolation,

whether the physical isolation of the prisoner, the moral isolation of a friendless and misunderstood man, or the self-imposed isolation of the misanthrope. Isolation is actually a negative reality, but solitude is positive and existential. We may compare the relationship between the two to that between the unsought poverty of the proletarian and the voluntary poverty of the ascetic. Solitude, besides, is not ontological but moral. To claim an absolute and ontological solitude would be equivalent to saying that nothing exists outside the self, a proposition which no sceptic idealist would dare to advance. The concept of absolute solitude has no more sense than that of absolute nothingness. As Bergson has shown that nothingness cannot be conceived of except in relation to being, so solitude exists only in relation to other human beings.

Experience also teaches us that solitude has no existential value if it is not accepted as a definite state, that is, unless it is seen as a *moment* in the existential dialectic which is fulfilled only by being superseded by another moment, superior to the first. As nearly all who have profited by it know, there is a great temptation to cease to consider solitude dialectically, and to take it as an absolute value. Now as man cannot endure total and prolonged solitude, he starts to use himself as an object of contemplation and to admire himself, like Narcissus. Freud says that in narcissism the ego takes itself as object of its libido, finding in it a pleasure surpassing any social relationship. In actual fact, however, this communion with self reveals not the richness of self, but its poverty and basic uncertainty. At this crucial moment two ways are now open to the ego: either to follow the example of Narcissus and make a supreme attempt at self-realization in suicide (whether physical or moral makes little difference), or else to find in his need an incentive to transcend solitude by the discovery of his fellowmen.

Dialectic and existential solitude always contains a longing for communication with other men and with the Absolute. There may have been hermits for whom communion with God alone was sufficient, but, even in the wilderness, most of them maintained spiritual contact with others, as for example, Père de Foucauld. Solitude reveals the existent to himself; but having thus discovered the extent of his weakness, the anguish which ensues leads him to desire to meet other existents, hoping secretly that they can help him to achieve the perfection which he has not been able to find in himself. Obviously it is not the abolition of his solitude which he seeks, since he is but too well aware of its benefits. He wants to transcend it, to change it into a higher form of being. The existent knows that no impersonal crowd, no superficial, objective relationship can transcend solitude without destroying it. What he needs for his self-realization is his fellowman as such, that is to say, as an existent who has also discovered himself in the anguish and joy of solitude.

To Christian existential philosophy goes the credit of having stated the problem of the fellowman in philosophical terms. As for atheistic existentialism, it sees the fellowman only as the non-self, the limit of self. Mystic writers like St John the Evangelist were the first to grasp the existential reality of the fellowman, insisting on this profound truth, that God does not reveal himself to man intellectually, but by personal communication with our soul, which he, as the absolute Other, initiates. Our philosophy of the fellowman is essentially evangelical in origin; it is through the Gospel that we learnt to consider our fellows not as objects for our use, but as persons whose dignity is on a level with our own. It is impossible to seek God, to love God except through the medium of our fellowmen, and consequently I cannot realize myself except through this same medium. Even on the psychological level we need our fellowmen in order to know ourselves, since we generally judge ourselves as others judge us.

The emotion which we feel at meeting another existent, is nearly always a mixture of hope and of fear. What will this being whom I have approached bring me? Will he tear me from my solitude only to cast me on to the trivial flood of everyday commonplaces? Or will his solitude join with mine so that ' he ' and ' I ' together form a new existential reality, ' us '?

Many modern philosophers, influenced by Hegel's idea of relations between human beings as a perpetual struggle, think that man does certainly desire to emerge from his solitude, but that the fellowman to whom he turns will never be anything except a rival, if not an enemy. Sartre, in particular, after what he calls an ' existential psychoanalysis,' considers that basically all human relationships are reducible either to indifference, sexual desire leading to the slavery of one to the other, or to hate. Love itself is only hatred in disguise. Our fellowman, consequently, instead of being a means of transcending our solitude, only reinforces it and makes us feel more than ever alone.

We cannot deny that the relationship between men is often, indeed, one of struggle, competition and rivalry. Nothing entitles us, so far, to say it is the only possible one. On the contrary, the generality of experience shows that if it is true that man too often acts ' like a wolf to his fellowman,' it is at least just as true that he can be a friend and helper. This is already so on the plane of social and objective relationships. The influence exercised by one man over another may certainly sometimes be a form of slavery; but how much more often is it our best way of defeating the inauthentic everyday? Because we came under the influence, at a certain moment in our life, of a particular man, either through his books or his art, or especially through direct contact with one whose prestige was based on truth, we awoke to the deepest aspirations of our personality, and conceived the project of realizing them. Weaklings are afraid of letting themselves be influenced by others. They fear that the only result would be a threat to their independence—independence which is more jealously prized the weaker the personality. A strong character knows that whatever he does, it is impossible to escape the influence of others; and consequently, rather than submit passively and more or less unconsciously to undesirable influences, he chooses, as far as he can, the influence he wants. This influence will then appear not as a compulsion but as an appeal, an appeal which comes to us through the intermediary of another, but from a source which is higher than either he or ourselves.

The most frequent form taken by relationship between people today is certainly free association, a concept which implies a community of interests and an opposition to another community of interests. There can be a real feeling of fellowship between those who do not know each other personally, or who are completely uninterested in each other as existents. Friendly societies, consumers' co-operatives, national and international trade union and professional federations and confederations, are some of the most usual forms of this anonymous, impersonal, but nevertheless very effective solidarity. One group of interests is nearly always at war with another group, since a certain amount of partisanship is an inherent part of the idea of solidarity. Nationalism is only conceivable in a civilization in which nations are, for various reasons, hostile to one another. Since such nations have begun to realize, thanks to ever-intensifying economic and cultural relations, the common nature of their interests, the feeling of national solidarity is beginning gradually to disappear, and only shows itself in fits and starts, like a kind of infantile neurosis whose roots are deep in the subconscious, a legacy of a dying civilization. After the first world war the altruistic founders of the League of Nations thought that it could embody a world-wide brotherhood. In this they seriously misunderstood the nature of solidarity. The League, being based on a mythical solidarity, could only fail. If at some future date mankind succeeds in reaching beyond the regional pacts which now link the various countries and achieves unity, it will only be by taking as a base some mystique far removed from that of solidarity.

It is undeniable, however, that within the bounadries of a single group bonds are formed which give the lie direct to the saying *homo homini lupus.* The class feeling of the proletariat, in particular, has given birth to acts of such generosity and unselfishness, even to the complete sacrifice of the individual, that it is not surprising that some Christian workers have confused it with the brotherhood of man preached by Christ. Malraux, for example, extolled the fellowship of comrades in arms, which is probably the most sublime form of human solidarity. The fact remains, however, that solidarity can neither end man's isolation, nor create an authentic inter-personal communion. It is not an existential, but a general bond. Even though they feel protected by belonging to a strongly class-conscious group or class, men still retain a profound feeling that they are strangers to each other. The mass man is not an existent, but a group-product; and as soon as he becomes aware of himself as an existent, he feels isolated and abandoned. ' Isolation,' said Kierkegaard, ' is produced where one is considered as a numeral. Where an individual is considered as an individual, his isolation is self-evident; but it is exactly the same isolation as when a hundred individuals are considered simply as a hundred.' Now, it is the coming together of a great number of individuals that creates solidarity. Each, within the limits of this solidarity, seeks his own advantage, which happens by chance to be the advantage of a certain number of others too.

I am not disputing the social value of solidarity. I would even admit that it is responsible for men being brought together, and thus increasing their chances of personal relations. If, however, solidarity is the only positive inter-personal bond, we should be forced to agree with Heidegger, who said that any encounter with other men can only increase the unhappiness of our consciousness, by causing the realization of its inevitable destruction and by depriving it of all the illusions which it could have forged in its solitude. We must look beyond the objective communication which solidarity brings.

The continual expansion of impersonal and social human relationships is not an answer to man's deep yearning for the re-establishment of that unity which was broken by sin. In the first stages of his existential evolution and spiritual development, man begins to realize the in-adequacy of objective communication and takes refuge in solitude. There he finds himself, but at the same time dis-covers in the depths of his being the need for a total, personal communion with other existents, equally conscious of their being. Here it is no longer a question of association for the purpose of material activities, or temporal advantages; we must transcend any thought of possession, and aim at the intimate fusion of two or several beings. Such communion will be founded not on the objective plane, but on the most profound inter-subjectivity. The other offers himself to me and I to him, resulting not in an objective community, but a new existential reality—' we.' ' We ' is not a simple addition of ' I ' plus ' you '; it is an original reality, infinitely richer than the ' I ' and ' you '; and in it this ' I ' and this ' you ' are enriched and their separate individualities enhanced.

It is obviously difficult to realize a communion like this. Were one of the existents to try to dominate or absorb the others, it could no longer be called existential communion. In the same way, if the ' I ' and ' you ' ossified into a state of mutual contemplation without aspiring towards Transcendence, it would again be false communion. Men can find communion only in something beyond themselves and, above all, in God. To fight against egoism, even egoism between two, is an indispensable condition of all authentic communion. If some atheistic existentialists have concluded that perfect communion is impossible and consider solitude, and consequently unhappiness, the only normal condition of existence, it is because existence for them is essentially egoism and not generosity. They cannot imagine that a man could give, and above all give himself, without being the poorer, nor that he could possibly want to do so. We must consequently look to existential analysis to tell us whether or not generosity is one of the basic characteristics of existence, and also whether a union between my inmost self and that of another is possible. While the deep-rooted natural desire for such union is a valuable indication, it is certainly not a proof of the possibility.

Should authentic communion between existents be

possible, we must look for it in love and friendship. For Karl Jaspers, it is true, existential communion is absolutely unique, unrelated either to love or to friendship. But Jaspers can no more define in what this unique reality consists than he can describe what he means by existence and by transcendence. Obviously all love and all friendship do not deserve to be called communion, but their own impetus, if sufficiently developed, will achieve it. Jaspers consequently would have been correct if we consider love and friendship as rough and inauthentic outlines of each other. If, as materialistic scientists tell us, love is only a psychic reaction to an aggregate of physiological stimuli, or an act which camouflages its animal nature with a haze of romantic poetry, it would obviously have no connection with existential communion. The same would be the case if human love was solely spiritual, ethereal and accessible only to a select few.

For me, as for a long tradition of spiritual philosophers beginning with Plato through St Augustine and Pascal up to Bergson, Blondel and modern Christian existentialists, love is the main motive-force of history, personal as well as collective. The need to love—*amare et amari cupiebam* as St Augustine said—is without question man's fundamental and most powerful ' instinct.' It is this instinct, and not, as Hegel and Marx thought, conflict, which forms the real dialectic of human evolution. Freud understood this, but as his materialistic prejudices prevented him from seeing the specifically spiritual element in love, he reduced it to sexual impulse. The more an existent spiritualizes himself —and only through love can this be achieved—the greater becomes his need to love. In the same way, if the lower forms of society are founded on objective communication, and especially on solidarity only love can serve as a basis for communities which bind together merely the temporal interests of individuals, but also their spiritual values of personality. This community already exists in the case of the family, at least as far as the evangelic message of Christ has penetrated. Should we, some day, construct a universal human society, one which did not characterize itself by opposition to other societies, it too could only be based on love. Obviously that day is still very far distant.

If my love aims at possessing or utilizing another, it is not existential, and will not lead to communion. Many misunderstandings would be avoided, if we were careful to distinguish between self-love and love. Sartre was not mistaken in denouncing the frequent camouflage of self-love as love, but he was quite wrong in reducing all love to self-love. Existentialist experience teaches us that not only a small élite, but most normal people have experienced a love which does not derive its own satisfaction from the utilization of the other, but positively and deliberately desires that the other should be himself, that in love they should remain themselves and find in it the promotion of their own selves. It is only when we concretely recognize the dignity and vocation of the other as a person, and that he exists not for us but for himself, that we can consider ourselves as being spiritually ready to love authentically. This applies as much to sexual love as to filial, parental, fraternal love and even friendship. Of all the various kinds of love, the love of parents for children is probably the hardest to make perfectly unselfish, because, especially in the case of maternal love, it is so deeply rooted in natural instinct, and this alone renders its spiritualization more difficult. The parents of an only child have particular difficulty in recognizing that he or she is an independent person, who must realize his or her own destiny. Under cover of an absorbing love, they prevent their child from becoming adult, and try if possible to keep him in a state of childishness.

Love, by putting an end to the egoism of the lover, releases the existence of self. If we feel the frustration of love more acutely than any other privation, it is because we know in our secret heart that love is essential to conquer our isolation. Love need not necessarily bring us happiness; we can be happy through being loved without loving in return. Suffering is not inherent in the idea of love either, and it is false to ascribe to it a masochistic character. We can, however, say that a love which has not yet been put to the test of suffering is uncertain; it may be no more than a passing physical attraction. In any case, only those whom we truly love can make us suffer. The most that others can do is to hurt us.

To be loved is, certainly, a great grace, and yet it is not being loved but loving which frees us from our egoism. Only mutual love, however, can create authentic existential communion. Perfect reciprocity is rare, it is true; it cannot be acquired, and is only sustained in constant and mutual effort. Experience teaches us that it does exist and, consequently, existenital communion is not a utopian dream. As love shares in the absolute love of God, it is inherently creative. Love can restore purity to one who has lost it, and we know by experience that in order that a man should cease being egotist and avaricious, he needs to know an authentic love. It is for this reason that the faults, even the worthlessness, of the loved one do not discourage the lover. He has the innate conviction that its creative power can triumph over it. If Christ, to the great scandal of the Pharisees, allowed himself to be approached by the woman who was to become St Mary Magdalene, but who was still only a woman of loose morals, it is because he knew in advance what a miracle his love was going to work in this soul thirsting for love. Only its own powerlessness can deceive love.

Contrary to a widespread prejudice, founded on the confusion between love and its by-products, love is not blind. On the contrary, there can be no existential knowledge except through its mediation. Cold, objective reason is excellent only for pragmatic knowledge, whereas even in the case of the true scientist or scholar, love of science or the results hoped for from research normally stimulate reason. ' We only learn to know,' said Goethe, ' what we love.' This is particularly true when it concerns knowledge of other people. As long as we do not love them, we will only know them superficially and impersonally. Love alone can give us intimate insight into what they are in themselves.

It is not the qualities of the beloved that we love. A father may be proud of the intelligence of a son, a fiancé delight in the beauty of his fiancée. These qualities may have led the way to love, but what we love in the loved one is their metaphysical reality. For this reason there is always something mysterious and inexplicable in all authentic love, we feel instinctively that to try to know why we love someone, or why he loves us, is an indiscreet and illicit betrayal, an attempt to reduce the mystery of love to the level of an intellectual problem.

Although love is a spiritual reality, it is deeply rooted in the psychic and moral structure of our being. Psychically, it is closely connected with admiration, and morally, it is inseparable from loyalty.

Women, especially, can love only men whom they admire. If they no longer admire, loyalty becomes meaningless and love dies. Reasons for such admiration obviously vary according to the quality and the degree of authenticity of the being. Primitive and vulgar people admire only physical strength and even, in perverted cases, the cruelty of the male, whereas for a cultivated woman moral, intellectual and spiritual qualities must be present before her admiration can be born or develop. When admiration is based on purely imagined qualities, or those without deep roots in the heart of the existent, it soon disappears, and is often replaced by active contempt, transforming love into hatred. Lovers should consequently never halt in their spiritual ascent, never accept mediocrity, and should always remain worthy of the admiration of the other.

Loyalty in love is not bounded by the merits of the loved one, nor is it a simple requirement of the positive moral law; it is inherent in the nature of love. The father of the prodigal son in the Gospel still continued loving him, even though his son had sinned and betrayed his filial loyalty. One lover's infidelity cannot justify that of the other.

Of all the prevalent popular beliefs about love the most mistaken is that which opposes love to liberty, and claims for it a kind of natural spontaneity—what we call a thunderbolt, but more durable. Actually, there is an intrinsic difference between love and instinct, and authentic love cannot exist except in a free act. As long as one being is in bondage to another, we cannot truly describe it as love. The physical attraction must be freely ratified by the mind. Only our own freewill can enable our love to prevail against obstacles, conquer its own imperfections, and transcend the inevitability of death.

If we use the word ' love ' without any qualification, it at once conveys the meaning of love between men and women, sexual love. This usage is unjustified, since love between parents and children, brothers and sisters, and between friends, ranks equally as a mediator in communion.

Love of philosophy, science and art also merits the title of love, and flows from the same inexhaustible fount of divine Love. It is, however, true that sexual love, the love between men and women, plays a particularly important rôle in the scheme of existence. More inherently passionate than other forms of love, it causes the harmonious union of the physical, psychic and spiritual forces of two beings, and thus gives rise to the deepest of all existential communion, in which the two existents are truly, as St Paul says, one flesh and one spirit. It is also obvious, however, that it is not just any sexual attraction which can play this part. What Freud and Sartre, for instance, call love is only a pale reflection of the authentic love that the great lovers of history knew, and innumerable couples know today. He who identifies love with the animal instinct of reproduction, an instinct which is itself very close to other natural human instincts, has no comprehension of the intrinsic and spiritual reality of love, and condemns himself to irrevocable solitude. It is, of course, quite true that the reproductive instinct is concerned only with the preservation of the species, and does not mediate any communion. Existence, however, while not militating against the species, is not subordinate to it. Authentic sexual love is a simultaneous and indissoluble spiritual and physical emotion, a practical proof of the essential union between mind and body. Recent works by Catholic moralists have emphasized this metaphysical character of sexual love, which the agapë, Christian charity, can transform by freeing it from its destructive and demoniac character.

Far from serving only the purposes of the species, sexual love confers a beauty and dignity on procreation which it cannot have as a mere result of instinctive copulation. The child born of love is the fruit of the flesh and the spirit, and it is love which strengthens and deepens the links of communion between married couples. But however important and necessary love is for procreation, it is not essential. The specific design of love is to support the creation of a community, an existential community. Consequently it is justified even when there is no question of procreation.

For me, however, communion in friendship is even more beautiful than communion in love. It is true that the fusion of the two existents is more complete in sexual love than in friendship. But it is just because sexual love is so deeply rooted in the carnal nature of man, that it is exposed to so many risks, and threatened by so many dangers. Friendship is more spiritual by nature, and more unselfish; and this enables us more easily to recognize its authenticity. Reciprocity in friendship is more perfect. We can imagine at least a temporary one-sided love, but friendship must be mutual. In the case of communion between a man and a woman, the ideal would obviously be that it should combine sexual satisfaction and friendship. It is, in fact, only when sex is united with friendship that it conquers jealousy and communion can transcend the couple and flow into the Universal.

Authentic friendship is free from jealousy and knows no bounds. Though it is normal to have one particular friend and a hierarchy in one's friendships, nothing is more false than to say that each of us can have only a single ' real friend ' at a time. Because friendship is based on mind, I can give myself completely, although in a different way, to each of my friends, and each one of them will share in the riches gained from my communion with my other friends. Besides, if the idea of a group of lovers is essentially depraved, a community of friends is not only possible, but imperative for the full development of friendship. And as, in theory, friendly communion is limitless, a truly universal society could be founded only on friendship. Lest such a society should become an anonymous monster, it should be composed of innumerable small communities of free people, since there is no friendship except between concrete beings with concrete relationships. In present conditions, such relationships are not a practical possibility except between a limited number of people.

Every human being, no matter how primitive or sophisticated he is, longs for friendship. Some people seem to have a sort of pre-established harmony which attracts them to each other. Long before they have any thoughts of sexual love, friendship comes to the hearts of children, just as it still links the old and infirm for whom ' love ' has long since lost all physical meaning. Most of the saints, following in Christ's footsteps, felt obliged to renounce sexual love, but nearly all—and in this also they followed the example of their Master—communed with their fellowmen in friendship.

As friendship is existential communion, it is the dialectic negation of the separated ego in order to arrive at the ' third term ' which is the existential ' we.' The essence of friendship is an ' I ' plus ' You ' relationship, in which the other is truly desired for himself. Long ago Aristotle stated that friendship presupposed a greater equality between the partners than sexual, parental, filial or fraternal love. There is, however, no need for material, cultural or spiritual equality between friends, since experience proves that there can be true authentic friendships between people belonging neither to the same milieu nor to the same social rank, and widely differing in means and education. But in no case should one friend dominate the other, nor treat him either as a superior or as an inferior. As friendship comes under the heading not of possessions, but of existence, it has no need of those goods which are not identified with the existence of the friend.

No communion is intrinsically less egoistic and more directed towards Transcendence than friendship. When two or more beings limit their spiritual ambitions to their relationship with each other, this is not friendship but simple camaraderie. Friendship always implies the urge to Transcendence; and more than any other existential communion takes its source from a reality which surpasses the friends themselves. This Transcendence may be art, philosophy, or some great patriotic or revolutionary cause; but it is above all their common communion in God, the absolute Transcendence, which raises the friends far above a closed ' we.' The man who says or thinks that ' man is a wolf to his fellowman ' is certainly one of those unfortunates who have never known authentic friendship. Even if, on my way through life, all except one of those I met, were base and egotistical, one single experience of authentic friendship would entitle me to take an optimistic view of human nature.

Friendship applies to the whole spiritual personality; it does not exclude the physical aspect of the friends, or sentimental effusion and tender attachment. There is, however, something virile in it, which is opposed to its degenerating into sentimentality. Intelligence plays a greater part in it than in sexual love, or even than in family love. In the case of educated people friendship is more likely to be seen in the sharing of a worth-while endeavour or in a common search for truth, than in sentimental effusions. There is, however, no technique or rule for success in friendship. The man who does nothing but wait passively, will probably never find it. We must prepare ourselves for friendship, we must open our hearts and minds to every opportunity of communication with our fellowmen, and be ready to receive their call when it comes.

Every communion can mediate further communion. My affection for my friend is a stage on the road to love of my fellowmen. The love of humanity reveals to me the links which unite me to the cosmos; cosmic communion leads me to him who is the Author and the Father of all. Conversely, it is by opening my mind to the infinite beauty of God that I can respond to the call of others who also admire and adore the supreme Beauty.

I myself have no doubt that authentic communion is possible between human beings. Existence is consequently not an abyss of desolation and hopeless loneliness. Existential experience, however, also teaches us that no human communion is absolutely perfect, or capable of completely satisfying our thirsting souls. In the heart of each existent there is a secret place, incommunicable and inaccessible to others. It is because most lovers and friends will not respect this ultimate privacy of their own ego and the ego of the other, that there are so many futile misunderstandings and so much suffering. In a certain sense we can even say that the more authentic the existential communion between two human beings, the greater is their longing for absolute communion. It would seem, then, that the chief purpose of human communion is to prepare us for, and lead us to communion with God, who is the Absolute. Only then will the existent attain complete perfection and see death no longer as a catastrophe, but as the ultimate realization of existence.

⚓ M. H. GILL AND SON LTD., PRINTERS, DUBLIN